GET IN
THE GAME

GET IN
THE GAME

8 ELEMENTS OF
PERSEVERANCE THAT MAKE
THE DIFFERENCE

CAL RIPKEN, JR.

WITH DONALD T. PHILLIPS

GOTHAM BOOKS

GOTHAM BOOKS
Published by Penguin Group (USA) Inc.
375 Hudson Street, New York, New York 10014, U.S.A.
Penguin Group (Canada), 90 Eglinton Avenue East, Suite 700, Toronto, Ontario M4P 2Y3, Canada (a division of Pearson Penguin Canada Inc.); Penguin Books Ltd, 80 Strand, London WC2R 0RL, England; Penguin Ireland, 25 St Stephen's Green, Dublin 2, Ireland (a division of Penguin Books Ltd); Penguin Group (Australia), 250 Camberwell Road, Camberwell, Victoria 3124, Australia (a division of Pearson Australia Group Pty Ltd); Penguin Books India Pvt Ltd, 11 Community Centre, Panchsheel Park, New Delhi – 110 017, India; Penguin Group (NZ), 67 Apollo Drive, Mairangi Bay, Auckland 1311, New Zealand (a division of Pearson New Zealand Ltd); Penguin Books (South Africa) (Pty) Ltd, 24 Sturdee Avenue, Rosebank, Johannesburg 2196, South Africa

Penguin Books Ltd, Registered Offices: 80 Strand, London WC2R 0RL, England

Published by Gotham Books, a member of Penguin Group (USA) Inc.

First printing, April 2007
10 9 8 7 6 5 4 3 2 1

Gotham Books and the skyscraper logo are trademarks of Penguin Group (USA) Inc.

LIBRARY OF CONGRESS CATALOGING-IN-PUBLICATION DATA
Ripken, Cal, 1960–
    Get in the game : 8 elements of perseverance that make the difference / Cal Ripken, Jr. with Donald T. Phillips.— 1st ed.
        p.   cm.
    ISBN 978-1-592-40264-9 (hardcover)   1. Ripken, Cal, 1960–   2. Baseball players— United States—Biography.   3. Baltimore Orioles (Baseball team)—History.   4. Perseverance (Ethics)   I. Phillips, Donald T. (Donald Thomas), 1952–   II. Title.
GV865.R47A3   2006
796.357092—dc22
[B]
                                                                2006027872

Printed in the United States of America
Set in Garamond
Designed by Mia Risberg

While the author has made every effort to provide accurate telephone numbers and Internet addresses at the time of publication, neither the publisher nor the author assumes any responsibility for errors, or for changes that occur after publication. Further, the publisher does not have any control over and does not assume any responsibility for author or third-party Web sites or their content.

CONTENTS

PREFACE

Lou Gehrig and I shared a connection that goes back to old-school values and principles about going to work every day and hanging in there when the going gets tough. It's the basic belief of simply rolling up your sleeves and doing the job to the best of your ability. Ideals such as these harken back to a time when baseball was just a game.

I remember being on the top step of the dugout with a bunch of other shortstops back at the 1998 All-Star game at Coors Field in Denver. Alex Rodriguez, Derek Jeter, Omar Vizquel, Damion Easley, and I were watching the home-run-hitting contest when Derek began asking me questions.

Derek Jeter was the starting shortstop for the New York Yankees. He'd been drafted out of high school in 1992, spent several years in the minor leagues, and had finally been called up to the majors in 1996. In his first full season, he had batted .314 and was named Rookie of the Year in the American League. He'd had another excellent year in 1997, and after starting 1998 like gangbusters, he had been selected for the All-Star summer classic.

You could have taken these basic facts about Derek's early career, erased his name, and inserted mine. It's almost exactly the same thing that happened to me. When I was voted into my first few All-Star games, I used them as wonderful learning opportunities, because I was with some of the game's best veteran ballplayers. So I hung around them, asked all kinds of questions, and listened to what they had to say. But in 1998, the shoe was on the other foot. Derek Jeter was twenty-four years old and appearing in his first All-Star game. I was almost thirty-eight and participating in my sixteenth summer classic. He was the kid and I was the veteran from whom he wanted to learn.

"How do you make only three errors in an entire season?" was the first question Derek asked me. We chatted for a few minutes about that one—about fielding, preparation, anticipation, and luck. And then Derek posed a question for which I didn't really have an answer:

"What's the secret of playing every day? How do you do it?"

I paused for a moment, then said, "You know, Derek, I just . . . I just play."

I can still remember the look on his face. It wasn't one of total disappointment. Rather, it was more of a puzzled look. I giggled a little bit and thought to myself that he either believed I didn't want to share my secret, or thought I wasn't very smart. Either way, I'm sure Derek expected me to give him a definitive answer: "This is what you have to do—a, b, and c." But at that point in my career, I couldn't really answer his question in such specific terms—even though others had asked me the same thing many times before.

Two and a half years earlier, on September 6, 1995, I had broken the major league baseball record for consecutive games played. On that day, I'd played in my 2,131st straight ball game, and up to the 1998 All-Star game, I had still not missed a single day of work. My streak would eventually end later that year, on September 20, 1998, after I had played in 2,632 consecutive games.

The man who'd held the record before me, Henry Louis Gehrig, was more than just a baseball player. He was an American icon, a legend. And I believe it's appropriate for anyone interested in perseverance to study the life and career of the Iron Horse, as he came to be known.

Lou Gehrig was born in 1903 to poor German immigrants. His parents had four children, but he was the only one to live past infancy. His mother was a cleaning lady and his father performed odd jobs. Together, the three lived in a cramped apartment in Manhattan. Growing up, Lou never missed a day of grade school. He was also a young athlete who played baseball, basketball, football, and soccer. After graduating from high school, he attended Columbia University on a football scholarship. But it was his prowess as a feared hitter of baseballs that garnered the attention of professional scouts. In 1923, over his mother's objections, Lou signed a contract with the New York Yankees and left college. In later years, he would state that his reason for doing so was simple. "My family needed the money," he said.

After spending a couple of years in the minor leagues, Lou

was called up by the Yankees and quickly became the team's star first baseman. Forever etched in baseball lore, Lou Gehrig was a member of the 1927 Yankees, which is considered one of the greatest teams in the history of the sport. His teammates included such baseball greats as Earle Combs, Waite Hoyt, Joe DiMaggio, and the great Babe Ruth. In contrast to Ruth, however, Lou was a modest man. Shy and reserved, he shunned the spotlight and was universally regarded as a nice guy. "There was absolutely no reason to dislike Lou Gehrig," wrote sportswriter Fred Lieb, "and nobody did."

During his fourteen-year career, from May 31, 1925, to May 2, 1939, Lou Gehrig played in 2,130 consecutive games. The streak ended only because he had contracted a devastating disease that prevented him from playing baseball to the best of his ability. Shortly after Lou took himself out of the starting Yankee lineup, he was diagnosed with amyotrophic lateral sclerosis (ALS), a disorder that attacks the body's motor-nerve cells and gradually causes muscles to weaken and waste away. There is no known cure, and it is usually fatal to patients within five years of being diagnosed. Lou was such a well-known and beloved sports hero that ALS quickly became known as Lou Gehrig's disease.

During the weeks and months leading up to September 6, 1995, when I eventually broke his record, there was a great deal of publicity, which included a resurrection of interest in Lou. The 1942 movie about his life, *Pride of the Yankees,* starring Gary Cooper, was shown many times on television, and there were countless newspaper and magazine articles written about him. I resisted reading or listening to most of the material, though, because I did not want to become obsessed with the streak, which might have changed my approach. What I was doing was working fine for me.

It wasn't until after I had retired from baseball that I began studying Lou's life and career—and I was amazed at the many parallels in our careers and how similarly he and I approached our jobs. Here are just a couple of examples:

I was a hometown kid—born and raised only thirty miles northeast of Baltimore, Maryland. I signed with my hometown team, the Baltimore Orioles, and spent my entire career with them.

> **Lou Gehrig was a hometown kid, born and raised on Manhattan's Upper East Side in New York. He signed with his hometown team, the New York Yankees, and spent his entire career with them.**

I skipped college and played for several years in the minor leagues before being called up to the majors. During that first full year with the Orioles, I cracked the starting lineup and stayed there for the next twenty-one years.

> **Lou Gehrig dropped out of Columbia University and spent several years in the minor leagues before being called up. During his first full year with the Yankees, he cracked the starting lineup and stayed there for the next fourteen years.**

While in the major leagues, I was known for my size. At six feet four inches and 225 pounds, I was the first "big" athlete to play shortstop regularly. I ended up hitting more home runs than the average player in that position.

> **While in the major leagues, Lou Gehrig was known for his size. At six feet, 200 pounds, he was acclaimed for his big shoulders, large biceps, and powerful legs. While playing first base, he hit many more homes runs than the average player in that position.**

Lou Gehrig and I shared another connection, I believe—one that goes back to old-school values and principles about going to work every day and hanging in there when the going gets tough. It's the basic belief of simply rolling up your sleeves and doing the job to the best of your ability. Ideals such as these harken back to a time when baseball was just a game, back to the days when big money and huge player salaries weren't really much of a factor in the sport.

I found it interesting that at Lou's retirement ceremony on July 4, 1939, not only did all of Lou's past and present teammates attend (including Babe Ruth and Joe DiMaggio), but the postmaster general of the United States also showed up. Postmen in the United States have long been regarded as having an unwavering commitment to performing their jobs, regardless of the adverse conditions they may encounter. Inscribed on the building of the New York City Post Office (near where Lou Gehrig grew up) is what has long been known as the Postman's Creed:

Neither snow, nor rain, nor heat, nor gloom of night stays these couriers from the swift completion of their appointed rounds.

This is not a value that began with the formation of the United States Postal Service. Rather, it is a direct quote from the works of Herodotus, which go back twenty-five hundred years to the ancient Greeks. It refers to the expedition of the Greeks against the Persians in 500 BC and describes the faithfulness and reliability with which the Persians operated their system of mounted postal couriers. Now that *really is* old school. But the idea behind the Postman's Creed is also an American value. You get up, you go to work, you do your job, and you try to do it to the best of your ability—and then you go home, get up, and start all over again the next day. Such a creed is admired everywhere by all hardworking, decent people.

Looking back on the events leading up to my 2,131st game, I remember people around the country relating the streak to their own jobs and careers. Newspapers and magazines were filled with individual stories of perfect attendance at work and school. There were hundreds of profiles about average citizens who hadn't missed a day of work in three, four, or five decades. *USA Today* held a national contest and eventually declared the winner to be a Chicago hardware-store owner named Herbert Christiansen, who had not missed a day of work since he'd begun the job back on April 1, 1936.

I found that to be almost unbelievable because, back then, Lou Gehrig was still playing first base for the Yankees and wouldn't retire for another three years. To top it all off, in my hometown of Baltimore, right under everybody's noses, we found that my upcoming 2,131st consecutive game would also mark Ernie Tyler's 2,180th straight game seated behind the backstop doing his job as the team's umpire attendant. Talk about a quiet, dedicated guy; Ernie was the best.

It just seemed that the groundswell leading up to my breaking of Lou Gehrig's record was never-ending. Everybody was talking about it in some form or another, in every industry and organization, in every corner of the United States. To tell you the truth, I was amazed at the sensation it generated. I also found it amusing that Pete Rose, who had retired back in 1986 with the most all-time career hits (4,256), actually went on record about my consecutive games streak, saying, "If I had known it was such a big deal, I would have done it myself."

In addition to hard work, another element of old-school values associated with my streak had to do directly with baseball. On August 12, 1994, major league players staged the eighth work stoppage in the sport's history. The dispute centered on ownership's demand for a salary cap, which was something the players' association would never accept. Unfortunately, the strike lasted 234 days, resulted in the cancellation of the play-offs and the World Series for the first time in major league history, and dragged on into the 1995 season. Finally, the next spring, a federal judge issued an injunction against the owners, and the season resumed on April 25,

1995, under the conditions of the previously expired contract.

After the strike was over, baseball fans everywhere were unhappy with how the sport had changed. Many people believed that greed had corrupted the national pastime. The owners wanted to ensure that their individual clubs would make a profit. The players wanted to preserve and protect the free market system. And the inability of the two sides to come together resulted in a painful, almost tragic suspension of the nation's national pastime. So when the 1995 season began, people were looking for something they could latch onto—something that offered hope for the future of baseball.

The buildup to September 6 and game number 2,131 was slow but steady. As my challenge to Lou Gehrig's record progressed, I believe people looked at me and thought, "This goes back to the way we used to see baseball, the way we remember baseball, back when it was pure, when it wasn't tarnished, when the players out there were our heroes. We wish all players were like Lou Gehrig and Cal Ripken—playing more for sheer love of the game than anything else."

> *"I really love the game, [and] hate to think of taking even one day off when we are playing. I hate to think of the inevitable time when I will have to hang up the spikes and put the uniform away."*
> **—LOU GEHRIG**

I sometimes wonder how many consecutive games Lou would have played had he not been afflicted with ALS—and if, in that case, I would ever have broken his record. Lou played in 2,130 straight games. I played in 2,632. It might have been close.

Some people say that no one will ever come near to playing in that many games again, and there seems to be a consensus that my streak is now one of baseball's unbreakable records. But that's what everybody said after Lou Gehrig retired. Sportswriters of the day called it "The Record That Will Never Be Broken." Columnist Shirley Povich noted that Lou's record was "long deemed as the most defiant to challenge, the most unassailable, [and] the most unapproachable." There's a lot of truth to that because, after all, Lou's record did stand for an astounding fifty-six years.

Now that I've retired, I'm often asked if I think the record will ever be broken. It's an interesting question. In this day of big money, priorities have changed for many athletes. Almost nobody plays for the same team over his entire career. Many players now have personal trainers, dedicated money managers, and specialized sports agents. Pressure from the media also seems to have dramatically increased, especially on an athlete who is nearing a record, or one who is even remotely controversial.

Do I think my consecutive games record can be broken? Yes, I do.

Playing 2,632 straight ball games and breaking Lou Gehrig's record was not all about extraordinary athletic talent. I didn't have a bionic body or a burning desire for the spotlight—and I tried not to make excuses for poor performances.

> *"I do not want to be a hero, and I would hate like hell to be a crybaby."*
>
> —LOU GEHRIG

Still, many times the streak was seriously threatened. The Baltimore Orioles, for instance, only made the play-offs three times during my career. And when you're the starting shortstop for a team that doesn't win, your job is always in jeopardy. Even though I stayed with the O's for my entire career, I was tempted to leave one time when upper management fired my dad as manager. There were also many injuries over my career. I endured muscle pulls, ankle sprains, twisted knees, and back problems. I was hit by pitches, participated in on-field brawls, wrestled in clubhouse high jinks, got banged up in pickup basketball games, and collided with catchers at home plate more times than I care to remember. I was lucky that I didn't get injured seriously enough that I would have been forced to sit out a game.

> *"Ty Cobb once told me something after he retired. 'To last a long time,' he said, 'you've just got to be lucky enough to avoid serious injuries.'"*
>
> —LOU GEHRIG

When I went into slumps, I was booed. And when I insisted on staying in the lineup, I was termed "selfish." But I always believed that, even if I was less than 100 percent, there was some contribution I could make to the team. In fact, some of my best games were when my expectations were a little lower and I ended up pushing myself to perform. So I learned that perseverance sometimes pays off in ways that you least expect.

After I retired in 2001, people began asking me to speak at various forums. And of course, they all wanted to know my "secret" to success. It was the same question Derek Jeter had asked me back at the All-Star game in 1998. The absolute truth of the matter, however, is that I never felt I had a "secret." I just played baseball because I loved the game and because I had been taught certain values and principles that prevented me from backing away from anything. The streak was a result of who I was, how I was raised, and how I developed over the years. Still, though, when I went out and spoke in public, I wanted to be able to tell people something more.

So I began to think in depth about my streak. Eventually, I realized that much of it was about learning along the way. Over the years, I gradually increased my perception about how the game of baseball was played and what I should do, both as a shortstop and as a member of the team. The application of that acquired knowledge drew people to me and increased my value to the organization. More than that, however, the streak, I believe, was a matter of perseverance. It was about steadfastness, hanging in there in the face of difficulty, overcoming obstacles, and being there to perform the job I had been hired to do.

From there, I began analyzing the details of perseverance that applied to my situation. In due course, I came up with eight elements, which I found somewhat ironic because the number I wore on my back for those twenty-one major league seasons was 8. The eight elements discussed in this book are (1) The Right Values; (2) A Strong Will to Succeed; (3) Love What You Do; (4) Preparation; (5) Anticipation; (6) Trusting Relationships; (7) Life Management; and (8) The Courage of Your Convictions. I believe all eight elements can be applied in your business life, your personal life, or in whatever long-term endeavor you might wish to pursue.

In the forthcoming chapters, you'll see that I came up with three principles to explain each element in more detail. I've tried to explain things using my own voice, my own way, with a lot of baseball terminology. After all, that was my world. You, as the reader, can make the bridge to your world.

During my career as a major league ballplayer, I carried in my briefcase an inspirational quote by Theodore Roosevelt:

Far better it is to dare mighty things, to win glorious triumphs,
even though checkered by failure, than to rank with those
poor spirits who neither enjoy much nor suffer much,
because they live in the gray twilight that knows
neither victory nor defeat.

Every once in a while, I would pull out the quote and read it. I found it motivating. It spoke to me because I always felt that, by being on the sidelines, I could not experience life to its fullest. If I wasn't in the game, I couldn't win. And even though I might lose by being in there, I still felt that the risk was worth the reward. After all, losing is not only a part of baseball, it's a part of life.

Because I broke Lou Gehrig's fabled record, Derek Jeter and others thought I had a secret. But I really didn't. I played baseball the way I did all those years because that's the kind of person I am and that's how I was raised. It was simply who I was.

The bottom line for me was that it was just no fun not being in the game. Early in my career, when I sat on the bench, I felt that I was on the outside looking in. I was like the little boy who is sick in bed with a fever and has to look out at the other neighborhood kids playing a game in the street. It's the most torturous thing in the world to look out and watch everybody else enjoying himself when you can't be out there.

I didn't want to be that kid, looking out and seeing people having fun without me.

I wanted to get in the game.

During my twenty-one years in major league baseball, I played at six feet four inches and 225 pounds. But I wasn't always that big.

As a freshman in high school, when I tried out for the varsity baseball team, I had to stand on a scale and be weighed in front of everybody. It was embarrassing for me not only because I was clothed only in my underwear, but because I was the smallest guy in the locker room. The older players laughed and the coaches grinned when my stats were read aloud: "Ripken, five feet seven inches, 128 pounds." I'm sure I surprised them all, though, when I made the team's final cut. Even though I was physically overmatched, I could play solid defense at second base—and they were in dire need of a second baseman who could turn the double play.

That season, I batted ninth on a team that wasn't very good. My

---

batting average was only .128, and I was told to bunt so many times that I had to look carefully at the third base coach to make doubly sure that the bunt sign wasn't on. I know we lost a lot of games, but the thing I remember most about that season was the point system implemented by the coaches. It was a penalty of sorts for not doing well. Each player was graded during every game. If you got a hit, you were awarded four points. A great play in the field was worth two points. Every error, however, was worth minus two points, as were strikeouts. And that's the way it went—plus points for good plays, minus points for bad ones.

Before the first practice after each game, you had to take a lap around the football field for each negative point accumulated. If you'd had a really bad game and ended up with minus five points, you had to run five laps. Nobody liked to start out by running laps. But I'm sorry to say, because we were a lousy team, most of us were always running around the football field before practice.

I recall one time when I thought I'd done fairly well in a game. A bunt single and a couple of stellar defensive plays in the field, I figured, would surely offset two strikeouts at the plate. My optimistic calculations put me at plus two for the game. So when we assembled for practice the next day, I was feeling pretty good. Unfortunately, the coach didn't see the game the way I saw it. When he got to my name on the list, he yelled out, "Ripken, minus one! Take a lap."

"Minus one?" I thought. "Take a lap?" Even though I was stunned, I didn't argue. I just dropped my glove and took off.

CHAPTER 1

THE RIGHT VALUES

In order to be successful and persevere in anything, it all starts with the right values. You do the hard work. You do it with excellence. You are honest, sincere, and you give it your all.

W hen I was a kid, my dad used to come into my room early on weekend mornings, tap me on the knee, and say, "I need your help today." Usually, he'd do the same to my brothers, Fred and Billy, and our sister, Elly. Sometimes, it was just one or two of us. Of course, all we wanted to do was sleep in because it wasn't a school day. But when Dad tapped, we'd have to get up and go outside to help him do yard work. Usually we'd be on our knees pulling weeds out of the garden, cutting grass, and raking it all up. When we got down to the smallest amount of stuff, he showed us how to use our fingers as a rake so the smallest clippings would not be left behind.

Periodically, our designated task was to trim out the driveway. Rather than using a Weed Eater or an electric edger, our tools consisted only of a hatchet and a string. Expenses were tight and Dad worked three different jobs. But we weren't deprived. We lived in a nice house. So I often wondered if we couldn't afford the more expensive tools, or if this was just the way Dad preferred it. At any rate, on each side of the driveway, we'd put down a line anchored by two nails. Then we'd get on our hands and knees and use the hatchet to make angled chops against the concrete. I can still remember finishing the job, standing up and looking at the driveway, and thinking how good it looked.

We didn't always have the best tools to do the project, but we always had the best intentions of completing our task and doing it well. While I longed for a nice wheelbarrow, we used an old wagon that Dad reinforced with steel strips to make it strong enough to carry rocks. While everybody else seemed to have crisp, new lawn mowers, ours were always old and refurbished. I remember one time I was riding with my father when he saw a mower in the trash at the top of the hill. He quickly stopped, backed the car into the driveway, and went up and knocked on the door. "Are you throwing that out?" he asked.

"Yeah, sure am," came the response.

"Mind if I take it?"

"Nope. Help yourself."

Then Dad took the mower home, tore it apart, put it back together, and got it running again. And we used that mower to cut our lawn. That's just the way it was with my father.

Even after I made it to the big leagues, I bought him a brand-new pickup truck. But he still preferred to use an old, beat-up red trailer hooked to his car to haul mulch and other materials. I guess he just felt he already had the right tool for the job.

HARD WORK

My father was a worker, a doer. He didn't dream and he didn't wait. He taught me at an early age the importance of hard work, ingenuity, and getting the job done. And to this day, when it comes to perseverance, I believe a hard-work ethic is indispensable. Without it, the odds go down you'll finish what you start. But a reliable, energetic, and determined work ethic greatly increases your chances of success at any endeavor, in any field.

Lou Gehrig and I are tied together with a consecutive-games streak. The most important trait we had in common, I believe, was a hard-work ethic. Lou once copied down three maxims that had to do with hard work. He tried to live by them:

1. Strive and succeed.
2. Early to bed, early to rise.
3. Labor conquers everything.

For me, hard work was not so much a lesson learned as it was a way of life. When I was a kid, it was just the way we did things in the Ripken household. If I missed a trash day, for instance, all hell would break loose. It made no difference that the trash bin might only be half-full. What mattered was that the trash had to be taken out on the day it was picked up. Mom and Dad also both believed in that old saying "Idle hands are the devil's workshop." Nobody ever just sat around when I was a kid. On rainy days when there was nothing to do, Dad would take us out to the garage to sort nuts and bolts. He'd have us match them up by sizes, organize them, and put them in jars or coffee cans.

I was taught that if something I was doing didn't work out quite right, then I just had to try something different and carry on. When I first began playing Little League baseball, for instance, Dad was a catcher in the Baltimore Orioles minor league organization. To please him, I tried to be a catcher, too. But I wasn't well suited to that position. For one thing, I was such a skinny kid that the gear never seemed to fit. It was always either way too tight or way to big. So I gravitated toward the middle-infield positions.

By my junior year in high school, when I began growing like a weed, my coaches played me almost exclusively at either shortstop or pitcher. At this point, I remember Dad pulling me aside to tell me that he thought I was good enough to be drafted into professional baseball, if that was what I wanted. By my senior year, I had become a dominant high school pitcher, and my batting average constantly hovered around .500.

When a person grows up being active and working hard, those habits just naturally carry over into his adult life. And that's the way it was for me when I entered professional baseball. I was a highly scouted and sought-after high school prospect, and there was always a big stir when people came to see me play. But most of the scouts ignored my fielding and batting skills because they were more interested in me as a pitcher. Baltimore and Kansas City were the only two teams looking at me as a possible everyday player. And that's what I wanted to do for one basic reason: Infielders get to play every day, but pitchers do not. Fortunately, the Orioles drafted me and gave me a chance to be a shortstop. And that's when I applied my hard-work ethic.

Physically, I was in great shape, and mentally, I was stubborn. So I would never let anyone come in and outwork me. If I was taking ground balls side by side with a player who wanted the same job I did, that guy would have to quit before I did. I stuck with that rule for my entire career, from the minor leagues all the way through my twenty-one seasons in the majors. I must admit, though, that in later years, when I was forty-one years old and taking ground balls with twenty-one-year-olds, I really paid the price for my stubbornness. Many times, I would stay on the field until the younger guys went into the clubhouse. Then I would linger in the locker room until they left the ballpark altogether. Finally, I would fill up the whirlpool with ice and soak my aching body.

During all my years playing major league baseball, I never took for granted that I had a job. I worked hard day to day, month to month, and year to year to earn my position in the starting lineup. I believe most good people work hard. They do their jobs, they do what they're told, they're loyal to their organization, and they care about the work they do and the people around them. But I think we all know that hard work, alone, does not guarantee success. In many large organizations, we see too many people get ahead for the wrong reasons. They kiss up, brownnose, take too many days off, call in sick, take two-hour lunches, and spend too much time at the coffee bar. Too often, we see people promoted for something other than performing their job well. While most of us believe that good work should be the primary factor in an individual's success, reality tells us that this is just not always the way it works.

Despite that fact of life, I firmly believe that success starts with hard work. You cannot persevere in anything unless you are willing to put in the hours. I learned this primarily from my father. "If you didn't want to work, you shouldn't have hired out," he would say. "Don't just talk about it, do it!"

I didn't realize it until many years later, but when my father tapped my brothers and sister and me on the knee on weekend mornings and asked us to help him with the yard work, he never sent us outside by ourselves. He was always right there, on his hands and knees, doing the work right along with us. Dad taught us not only by his words, but also by his actions.

I was raised on hard work. It's the only way I know.

EXCELLENCE

I was also raised to do the best I possibly could on any job I took on. "If it's worth doing, it's worth doing right," Dad would say. "Why are you even going to attempt it if you're only going to do it halfway?" And once again, Dad taught us this value by doing it himself while we were working with him.

During the winters after a big snowfall, Dad would take Billy, Fred, and me out to shovel the sidewalk. Some of our neighbors would shovel only a narrow path, just enough to walk through. But not us. We had to shovel to the edge of the walk, so that when the snow melted, the sidewalks would look neat and perfect all the way around. And it was the same way with the driveway. We ended up shoveling a lot more snow than most of our neighbors. But Dad didn't stop there. He'd actually start clearing the sidewalks and driveways in the neighborhood if people hadn't yet gotten around to doing it. Dad did this, in part, to be a good neighbor. He figured that one good turn deserved another. Because he was away so often during the spring and summer, he was setting up a pattern where he knew that our neighbors would help out his family if something should come up while he was out of town.

My father's entire baseball career was spent in the Baltimore Orioles organization. He played minor league ball, scouted, coached, and eventually managed for them. So as a kid growing up in Aberdeen, Maryland, I couldn't help but be an Orioles fan. And my favorite player, by far, was the great third baseman Brooks Robinson.

Brooks was in the Orioles lineup almost every day. In fact, he owned the Orioles record for consecutive games played at 463. Actually, by the time he finished his career, Brooks held many major league records and most of Baltimore's individual records, including putouts, assists, chances, double plays, and fielding percentage. He was such a legend that he became known as Mr. Oriole. But the main reason I idolized Brooks Robinson was for the way he played third base.

Known as the Human Vacuum Cleaner, or Hoover, he set a standard of excellence at his position that has never been surpassed. No one, I mean no one, in the entire history of baseball has played third base better. Brooks won sixteen consecutive Gold Glove Awards and played in fifteen All-Star games. He was perfection at third base, and I wanted to be as good as he was at whatever position I played. In Little League, when I made a great backstab on a grounder, I yelled, "Brooks Robinson!" When a kid bunted, I charged the ball just like Brooks. And when anticipating the situation in any given inning, I would always ask myself, "What would Brooks do?"

The standard of excellence set by Brooks Robinson exemplified the way the Baltimore Orioles played baseball. And because my father became a minor league manager with the organization, I grew up learning the "Oriole Way." From 1972 to 1974, for instance, Dad managed the AA team in Asheville, North Carolina. During those summers, I spent a lot of time at the ballpark. Before the games, Dad let me hit some balls and field some grounders. But when the players arrived, I had to move to the outfield to shag fly balls. That was the fun part for me, but it wasn't all I did—not by a long shot. Most of my time was spent doing the work Dad assigned me. Always dressed in my uniform, I sold candy at the concession stands, was the batboy during games, and performed a variety of odd jobs in the clubhouse afterward, including washing clothes and sweeping up.

One of my most important jobs was to shine the players' shoes (both visitors' and the home team's) so they would look good for the next day's game. Every pair had to be perfectly waxed, brushed, and buffed. If they weren't, I'd hear about it from my father, who personally inspected my work every single day. If, for instance, Al Bumbry's shoes didn't look the way they should, Dad wouldn't hesitate to say, "Not good enough, Son. Do them again." Al Bumbry would never complain about the job I did, even though he was a former military man who was particular about his shoes. Actually, I think he was happy he didn't have to shine his own shoes all the time. In later years, he told me that the only thing my father ever really asked of him was just to give him a good day's work.

The way my father ran his team was a picture of perfection. Jerseys had to be hanging a certain way in the locker, hats had to be right in the center of the upper shelf, shoes had to be spotlessly shined. Excellence was the underlying value in everything he did. "You know that old saying 'Practice makes perfect'?" Dad once asked me. "Well, it's wrong. *Perfect* practice makes perfect. I know that's a high standard to maintain, but it's the right way to do things. If you're taking ground balls, it's better to take fewer grounders and produce all the right repetitions than it is to take two hundred and just go through the motions."

My father wanted perfection in all aspects of baseball, especially in practice, because it built proper habits that would transfer over to the games. Even the most mundane drills can, if performed well, increase a player's chances of gaining a high level of perfection in virtually every aspect of the game. How my father conducted batting practice was a good example. When you stepped into the cage, you had to first lay down a few bunts. Then you had to slice a few to right field. That was the regimen he put in place, and I always felt I'd better adhere to it.

Dad ran batting practice in groups of four. Each time a group finished, a new pitcher and four new batters came in. The players who had just finished batting were responsible for picking up all the loose balls and running them out to the mound. Some guys dragged their bats behind them, grabbed one ball at a time, and casually walked out to the mound. But according to my father, that wasn't the right way to "clean the carpet," as it was called. "Put your bat down, run in there, pick up balls, and get off the damn field," he would lecture. "Minutes are ticking away and you're taking time away from the next group."

I grew up with the belief that there was a right way to do things and a wrong way to do things. And that it was the quality of the job that mattered most. Dad drilled into my head, "If you're going to do something, you might as well do it correctly."

"Some ballplayers have natural-born ability," Lou Gehrig once said. "I wasn't one of them."

Early in his career as a first baseman, Lou often looked clumsy and inelegant. But he understood that all the other in fielders counted on his defensive fielding abilities. He wanted to be excellent at his position so that his teammates could always rely on him. For that reason, Lou insisted on taking hundreds and hundreds of grounders and throws during practice. Balls skidded in the dirt, caromed off his shins and his chest, and broke the fingers in his throwing hand. Many of Lou's colleagues considered him something of a perfectionist. And after years of perfect practice, Lou Gehrig became one of the most reliable and valued fielding first basemen of his era.

Most people appreciate excellent work. Owners appreciate it. Managers and coaches appreciate it. Even teammates and coworkers appreciate it. It's been my experience that the only people who don't admire excellence in the work of others are those who are insecure, jealous, or have some self-interest in seeing a person perform poorly. Regardless of the task, if you complete it with the best possible quality and professionalism, it will usually result in people giving you positive references or simply asking you to continue what you're doing. That fact, alone, contributes to success in any industry.

Excellence is about building good habits. I always enjoyed doing a job or performing a task well. And I equally enjoyed looking back on my work, seeing the result, and then thinking, "Man, that makes me feel good. That was worth doing." I feel the same way in everything I do in life, not just baseball. And these early lessons my father taught were never forgotten. As adults, for instance my brother Billy and I used to share a town house in Baltimore. One winter after a major snowfall, the two of us went out and shoveled our sidewalks, our driveway, and then started on the neighbor's. At one point, we stopped, looked up, and grinned. Every inch of snow had been shoveled away. We had done the job just as Dad used to do it when we were kids.

Excellence in what you do is an important value, especially for those of us who have a conscience. You can't lie to yourself. If you look back and realize that you could have done better, it'll eat at you until you fix it. I don't do anything halfway.

HONESTY AND INTEGRITY

Both my parents were as honest as the day is long. My mother just wouldn't tolerate dishonesty of any sort. She also had strong principles and could be counted on in the clutch. Because Dad worked in professional baseball, he was gone most of the spring and summer. And because the rest of the family were anchored in Aberdeen, Maryland, Mom was responsible for all us kids. She was the one who made sure we were clothed, fed, off to school on time, and taken to the doctor if we got sick. During the summers when school was out, she was the one who loaded everybody in the car and drove us to Appleton, Wisconsin; Elmira, New York; Asheville, North Carolina; or wherever else Dad happened to be. There was never any question about it. Mom ran the show on the home front, and she didn't have time to deal with dishonesty from any of her kids. Lying was never, ever tolerated.

Dad was also as straight a shooter as they come. If you asked him a question, you got a direct answer. He had a strong sense of right versus wrong. And if he thought something was wrong, believe me, you heard about it. Dad also tended not to mince words. Nor would he stay quiet just to avoid telling you bad news.

So, just as with the values of hard work and excellence, my parents raised me to be honest and to have integrity. Because of them, I believe I grew up to be a sincere and serious-minded adult. But how do honesty and integrity help a person persevere? Personally, I think it has something to do with trust.

Honesty breeds trust in others. Straight shooters get more work, are appreciated more, and are almost always respected. On the other hand, dishonest people almost never garner universal respect. As with honesty, integrity also breeds trust. If people believe you have strong principles, are sound in mind and body, and are incorruptible, they'll choose to work with you over others.

You cannot persevere in any organization without the trust of others. If an executive doesn't trust you, you can be out of a job in the blink of an eye. If coworkers don't trust you, they'll complain about you behind your back. And too much of that can also lead to a lost job. It's far better to be trusted by the people with whom you work and associate. But, as the adage goes, trust has to be earned. Only over a sustained period can people come to count on you. You have to demonstrate your honesty and integrity over and over. And you can't slip up—not even once. If you do, you have to start all over again. In that case, it's doubly difficult to regain a person's respect and esteem. Therefore, it's always wise to start out being straight with people from day one. Let them know right from the beginning that you can be counted on to give your all and perform your job to the best of your ability at any moment, in any situation, every single time. That's integrity.

The way I translated this value to baseball was simply to play every game as if were the most important one of the season. Early in my career, sportswriters mentioned that I leaped and lunged for balls, that I always slid in hard at second base when a double play needed to be broken up, and that I ran all out on the base paths. Late in my career, as I was closing in on Lou Gehrig's record, those same writers questioned why I didn't want to prolong the streak by playing one inning a game or becoming a DH (designated hitter). The truth is that I never played a single game with the idea of preserving my consecutive-games streak. I felt that, had I done so, I would have been disrespecting the game of baseball. I would also not have been able to look myself in the eye. So I played all out—all the time. To me, that was a big part of my personal integrity. Dad taught me to approach whatever I did in life correctly and to the best of my abilities. I simply cannot do anything less. It is part of who I am as a person.

> *"There is no excuse for a player not hustling. I believe every player owes it to himself, his club, and to the public to hustle every minute he is on the ball field."*
> **—LOU GEHRIG**

. . .

IN ORDER TO BE SUCCESSFUL and persevere in anything, you have to start with the right values. You do the hard work. You do it with excellence. You are honest, sincere, and you give it your all. To me, that is an honest and pure approach— one that helps you meet the challenges of the day.

Throughout my career, when things got complicated, when I hit some bumps in the road (such as losing streaks or personal slumps), I would sit down and ask myself, "What do I do? Should I continue to push forward? Should I take myself out of the lineup?"

During those times I fell back on my basic values. At first, I thought long and hard about exactly what those values were. Then, when I experienced another slump, I sat down and wrote out a simple statement so that I could refer to it later. Some people might equate this to a personal mission statement or outlining strategies and goals. For me, though, it wasn't really that involved. All I wanted was one sentence that described my job. And as you might imagine by now, I fell back on something my father had told me when I was struggling in the minor leagues. "Your job as a baseball player is to be prepared every single day, to come to the ballpark ready to play, and if the manager chooses you, you play." It was that simple.

You'll notice that this statement does not mention the key values that I have always fallen back on. That's because hard work, excellence, honesty, and integrity have become so ingrained that they are actually part of who I am. I now take it for granted that these values will be present in *everything* I do. They are my foundation for life—something from which to build.

When you possess the right values and live by them, good habits become routine. Communicating with people while at work is a good example. When Dad and I went outside to do yard work, he used that time together to talk to me about things of substance, about life, and about the decisions we made as we were growing up. It was similar to conversations another family might have around the dining room table. Only my father did it while we were working.

I remember one time when I was about sixteen or seventeen years old and Dad tapped me on the knee at about 7:00 A.M. "Come on, Son," he said, as usual. "I need your help today." He was well aware that I had come in late the night before, maybe around one or two in the morning.

For the first twenty minutes that we were on our hands and knees pulling weeds, neither of us said a word. Finally, out of the blue, Dad said something like "Came in a little late last night, didn't you?"

There was a long pause until I finally murmured, "Uh-huh."

"Why is it so hard to come in on time?" he asked.

Another pause. "Well, my friends don't have to be in that early and it's hard for me to speak up and tell them," I finally responded.

Dad had sparked a conversation that promoted dialogue back and forth. He listened to what I had to say, and then he gave me his perspective on the situation. Our conversation didn't last long, and because we were pulling weeds, it didn't feel painful, as if I were being chewed out. Afterward, however, when I was out with my friends, I started coming in on time.

At that young age, the wisdom with which my father approached that situation didn't really resonate with me. But over the years, as I have reflected on it, his choice to communicate words of importance while we were working together really made a lot of sense. And I would employ that method myself when I became an adult. I got in the habit of talking to my teammates, my coaches, my managers, while on the job. If something was bothering me, or if something was just wrong, I got it out in the open. And almost always, my coworkers responded in kind. I learned that I just had to take the initiative to open up a dialogue. And in the long run, I'm certain it fostered stronger teamwork and better working relationships in the organization.

With the right values, you develop good habits. And by developing good habits, with time you learn to do things on your own.

When I was seven or eight years old, Dad would drive the team's black station wagon crammed with the pitching machine and all the other baseball gear and equipment down to spring training in Florida. In the old days, that station wagon was the equivalent of today's modern tractor-trailer trucks. Just before Dad set out on his long drive, he insisted that we kids help him vacuum the inside of the car so it looked crisp and clean before he left. When I griped that the car was just going to get dirty on the drive, Dad smiled and said, "Well, I guess I'll just have to vacuum it out again when I get to Florida."

The next year, I noticed that my father had not vacuumed the car even though he was set to leave the next day. When I asked him about it, I could tell he was extremely tired. "Oh, it's not that bad. We'll just leave it." So, as a surprise for him, later that night I went down to the garage and vacuumed the car by myself. I still get emotional when I think of his reaction when he saw what I had done.

There are certain times when you're dad is pretty proud of you.

EIGHT RIPKEN PRINCIPLES

---

1. THE RIGHT VALUES

1. When it comes to perseverance, a hard-work ethic is indispensable. It increases your chances of success at any endeavor, in any field.
2. Never let anyone outwork you. Do not take for granted that you have a job.
3. If you don't want to work, you shouldn't have hired out. If it's worth doing, it's worth doing right.
4. Set a standard of excellence at your position. Remember, perfect practice makes perfect.
5. Be a straight shooter. If you're asked a question, give a direct answer.
6. Honesty and integrity help a person earn trust. You cannot persevere in any organization without the trust of others.
7. Integrity is being counted on to give your all and perform your job to the best of your ability at any moment, in any situation, every single time.
8. Play every game as if it were the most important game of the season.

After being drafted out of high school and spending three years in the mi-
nor leagues, I was invited to my first big league spring training camp in
Miami. But as soon as I got there, Earl Weaver, the Orioles' field man-
ager, gave me a heads-up that there was no real chance of me making the
club. I understood why. In 1981, the Orioles had a strong team, and they
were particularly set at third base (the position I was now playing) with
veteran Doug DeCinces.

Sure enough, when the first round of cuts was announced, I was sent
back to the minors. But because I had three days to report, I asked Earl
if it would be all right for me to stick around and use the facilities.
"Sure," he replied. "Stay as long as you want."

So as that day's exhibition game was getting started, I went down to

---

the batting cages in the corner of Miami Stadium to take some cuts. Almost immediately, though, a brisk wind blew the ball inside and caused me to swing my bat quicker than normal. I felt a twitch in my right shoulder and experienced some real pain. The team doctor diagnosed my injury as a strain in the point of my shoulder, gave me a cortisone shot, and ordered me to rest.

When I reported to minor league spring training, the only thing I was allowed to do was run with the pitchers. Unfortunately, some of my teammates believed that I was "big leaguing it" or pulling an "attitude muscle." "Ripken is just hacked off that he was sent down," they said. "He conveniently had this injury so he doesn't have to work like the rest of us."

I had to endure that sort of talk right up to the final several days of spring training when the team doctors and trainers told me that I'd have to start the season on the disabled list.

"What? The DL?" I protested. "Even before I get started? That wasn't part of the deal. I did what you guys told me to do. I didn't hit or throw, I got treatment every day, and I stayed in shape. Heck, we haven't even tested the shoulder to see if I can play."

"Okay, okay," they relented. "Let's test it and see where you stand."

When I started batting practice, rather than swinging full bore, I started "flicking" the bat just to make some contact. After all, I didn't want to aggravate the injury if it hadn't healed properly. Pretty soon, I was making some good contact and the ball was jumping off my bat. This was the first time my teammates had actually seen me taking batting practice, and when they noticed what I was doing, they realized that I really did have an injury. I was then allowed to play in the last few games of spring training and, now at game speed, I belted three or four solid hits without experiencing any pain.

After watching me hit and throw, the medical staff decided to let me begin the regular season. If I did well in the first week, they said, I could avoid going on the disabled list. Well, in my third at bat on opening day, I hit a home run. After that, they said I was good to go. Overall, I was glad I stood up for myself, because I got up to a great start in Rochester and, later that season, I was called up to the major leagues.

CHAPTER 2

A STRONG WILL
TO SUCCEED

Pitchers only get to play one out of five days.
I want to play every day.

In 1978, while still a senior at Aberdeen High School, I was selected by the Baltimore Orioles in the second round of baseball's amateur draft. Actually, I was number forty-eight overall, and the Orioles' fourth pick. On the whole, I was still thrilled to have been drafted by my hometown team.

The signing process took about a week and, during this time, my father helped work out decent contract terms. I didn't find out until later, however, that the Orioles organization had been divided about what to do with me. Hank Peters, the farm director, and Tom Giordano, the scouting director, wanted me to pitch. But Earl Weaver and Dick Bowie (who had originally scouted me) had seen me take batting practice and favored me as an infielder. That way, they thought, the team could have the benefit of my bat in the lineup every day.

Because of the disagreement, a meeting was called for Hank, Tom, and Earl to iron out a final resolution. My father was asked to sit in because he was one of Earl's coaches. The impasse was finally broken when Dad diplomatically suggested a compromise. "Look," he said, "in my experience developing kids in the minor leagues, we always start them out as regular players. If they fail, it's much easier for them to go back to pitching. But it's very difficult to do it in reverse." Then he suggested to the other three guys that they invite me into the meeting and ask for my opinion. After all, it was my career they were talking about.

"We just can't decide whether you should be developed as a pitcher or an infielder," said Hank, when I came into the room. "Cal, what do *you* want to do?"

"Well, I sure appreciate you asking, Mr. Peters," I replied without hesitation. "That's an easy decision for me. Pitchers only get to play one out of five days. I want to play every day."

"All right, son" came the reply. "We'll start you out as an infielder."

The next day, June 13, 1978, I formally became a member of the Baltimore Orioles when I inked a contract for $500 a month and a $20,000 signing bonus. And shortly after graduating from high school, I was in Bluefield, West Virginia, playing pro ball in the rookie-level Appalachian League.

Looking back on my professional career, I often think back to that first key decision. The truth is that I never pitched one inning in professional baseball—not in the minors or the majors; not even in blowout games. If I hadn't made the choice to play every day, I would never have broken Lou Gehrig's record.

> Lou Gehrig started out as a pitcher. But shortly after he signed a contract with the New York Yankees to play professional baseball, he was moved to first base. The manager believed Lou could hit so well that it would be much better for the team if he played every day.

AN INTERNAL DRIVE TO ACHIEVE

I'd like to say that my desire to play baseball every day was only because I loved the sport. But it was more than that. I also had a deep-seated desire to get things done, to achieve, to win. It was like a fire burning inside that propelled me forward. I don't know if such a force is totally genetic, or if it's learned in some way. Perhaps a little bit of both. I do know that many successful people have experienced the same feeling. And I also know that I had it when I was very young, that I had it at the age of seventeen when I signed my contract with the Orioles, and that I had it for twenty-one major league baseball seasons. As a matter of fact, now that I'm retired and embarking on an entirely new career in business, I still have it.

When I was a kid, this feeling was like a powerful force inside my body. It pervaded everything I did and caused me to be unusually emotional. In sports, I was the worst winner and the worst loser on the planet. It was never enough to finish second. If things didn't go my way, I'd get angry and throw temper tantrums. Many times in Little League, I would throw my bat against the fence or my helmet down on the ground. When I won, I would roam around the house bragging and boasting. "I'm like Muhammad Ali," I'd say. "I am the greatest!" Of course, that caused a lot of family arguments. Sometimes my brothers and sister and I fought like cats and dogs.

Mom and Dad were concerned about the emotional outbursts that were fueled by my internal drive. But rather than punishing me, they looked at my passion as more positive than negative. "That's a good thing," they would say. "It means you really care. So let's tap into that strong will and channel it in the right direction."

"How do I do that?" I asked.

"Well, instead of throwing a helmet or getting into a fight, do push-ups until you can't do them anymore. That way, you're putting your internal energy to use. You're exercising and building your upper-body strength."

I took my parents' advice to heart and tried to channel my energy and aggressiveness. But mastering that strong will took years. When I reached the minor leagues, for instance, I sometimes still got mad when things didn't go my way. But more often than not, rather than throw tantrums, I'd hold it in until after the game, when I'd do push-ups, take extra batting practice, or jog until I couldn't jog anymore.

Once I made it to the major leagues, the level of competition was higher, more meaningful, and more intense. As a result, it tended to put players on the brink of being out of control—and sometimes things would spill over. That's one reason beanballs, brawls, and heated arguments with umpires are a part of major league baseball.

> Lou Gehrig wanted to win. Some who knew him described him as having an obsessive nature, especially when it came to baseball. "I have the will to play," he once said. "Baseball is hard work and the strain is tremendous. It's pleasurable, but it's tough."

Here again, my father, a longtime baseball professional, came to the rescue. He taught me how to use my emotion as a motivational tool. "Anytime you get near the spillover point," he said, "take your internal energy and apply it against the other team. Beat them on the playing field. The way to get back at a pitcher who throws at you is not to charge the mound. Rather, you should pick yourself up, dust off your uniform, and hit one right back through the box."

Dad's suggestion really resonated with me. With time, I learned to channel my internal energy in the right direction. But it was always a bit of a struggle. I remember one time in the early 1990s when I was mired in a batting slump. I had failed for the umpteenth time in a row to deliver a hit for my teammates. Instead of punching something, I went into the training room and got on the treadmill. I recall Rick Sutcliffe coming in and out of the room a number of times wondering what in the world I was doing. It took me over an hour to burn off my negative energy. But at least I got a good work-out.

In 1995, after passing Lou Gehrig, I was mired in another batting slump when we traveled to Detroit for a three-game series. It was the end of the year, we were out of the pennant race, and in many people's minds there wasn't much to play for. But after I went hitless in the first game of the series, I grabbed a bucket of balls and went right back out to the field. I put a tee on top of home plate and started pounding ball after ball—first to center field, then left field, and then I began driving them into the seats. When the bucket was empty, I picked up every ball by myself. I must have hit two hundred or more balls that night.

My strong will to succeed not only became a powerful motivational force, but, with time, helped me overcome any fear of failure that might have invaded my thinking. A good example is how I performed in All-Star games over the years. The first few times I was selected to represent the American League, I was scared to death. I remember thinking things like "Just let me not make an error. I don't care if I don't get any hits. Just don't look foolish." So I took a conservative approach, and, as a result, I didn't do well in my first few summer classics. (I played in a total of nineteen All-Star games.)

In 1933, Lou Gehrig played in the very first All-Star game as the American League's first baseman. For the next five All-Star games, through 1938, he was the league's anchor at first base.

After a while, I remember asking myself, "What are you doing? To succeed, you have to be willing to take a chance. You can't be afraid to swing at a pitch in the dirt, because, after all, that's part of hitting."

Sure enough, after I changed my strategy, I started to perform better in All-Star games. I finally realized that to succeed I couldn't be afraid to fail. I had to throw caution to the wind and go for it. That's what getting in the game really means, I believe.

Now that I'm running my own company, I sometimes get frustrated with all the planning and meetings that take place. Strategy is important and I know we have to do it. But you can only plan so much. You can only prepare so much. At some point, you have to test your plans. I believe that many people are simply afraid to fail. So they don't even try. Perhaps I was conditioned by baseball, where, as a successful hitter, you fail seven out of ten times. Or perhaps my inner determination to succeed just kept propelling me forward. I don't know for certain. But I do know that my desire to take action has been a big part of my success.

Another thing I'm sure of is that, if I had not controlled my internal aggressiveness, it would definitely have affected my ability to play in 2,632 consecutive games. With a bad temper, I might have been thrown out of more games, suspended, or maybe even traded. I might have punched a wall, hurt myself, and been placed on the disabled list. But thanks to my parents, I learned how to channel that energy in a positive direction.

Five years after I retired from pro ball, my twelve-year-old son, Ryan, had a particularly bad Little League game and let loose with a flurry of emotion. In the car on the way home, I asked him what was going through his head at that moment. "I don't know," he responded. "It's just this thing. I don't know what to call it. I just get so mad."

I probably described that type of behavior the same way to my parents when I was twelve. A kid who's having those feelings doesn't know how to explain them or what they mean.

"That energy is not a bad thing, Son," I said to Ryan. "It's a good thing. It means you really care about the outcome of the game. You just need to learn how to control it."

I knew it would take time for my advice to resonate. It's a process. First come the words. Then you start to understand. You take some of the suggestions and try them out. Some of them work for you. Some don't. But always, you ask yourself, "How do I apply it? How do I apply it? How do I apply it?"

COMPETITIVENESS

I grew up in a very competitive family. In grade school, my sister, two brothers, and I were always trying to beat each other in a variety of activities. We played a lot of darts and Ping-Pong, for instance. And I recorded each game I won in a little black-and-white composition book. I would neatly write down the date, my opponent, and the scores of each game. "21–12; 21–10; 7–0; 11–1. Cal beats Billy all four games." It didn't matter that my brother Billy was four years younger. What mattered was that I beat him. Sometimes, before bed, I would open up my notebook and review my wins. It just gave me the greatest sense of accomplishment. There was no better feeling.

Unfortunately, that sense of euphoria became addictive. I just had to win. So I cheated all the time. But when I found myself cheating my own grandmother at cards, I paused and thought about what I was doing.

My father's mother lived with us for quite a long time when I was young. Even though she had lost most of her sight, she could still see well enough to teach us different card games. One of her favorites was canasta, where I quickly figured out that I could increase my chances of winning if, instead of only drawing two cards at a time (which was the rule), I drew four cards. Most of the time, I was sneaky enough to get away with it. But I believe that Grandma could see better than we were all led to believe, because she caught me a couple of times and really chewed me out.

Interestingly enough, it wasn't her anger that cured me of cheating. I still kept cheating at cards. But when I began to think about it, I realized winning that way didn't make me feel nearly as good as when I won legitimately. The truth is that cheating my blind grandma at cards wasn't very fulfilling. And I finally concluded that cheating was not a true measure of my skill. It was only a measure of how good I could cheat. After that, I never cheated anyone else again. Not at anything.

As an adult, I remained seriously competitive. I loved the competition in baseball, which exists in almost every phase of the game. There's team competition, individual competition, and an abundance of other competitive elements that you can experience only by being a professional. In the minor leagues, for example, I had to prove myself every step of the way. I had to show everybody that I was a better infielder than the player next to me. In that sense, each ground ball became a competition.

I continued to prove myself when I made it to the big leagues. Every time I went into spring training, a younger shortstop wanted to take my job. So I had to compete with each and every one of them. In the old school of baseball, when there was no such thing as financial security for players, the competitions for a particular position could get pretty ugly. Territoriality would set in and players could be down-right mean to each other.

But in the new school, most players take the approach that the guy standing next to them is part of their team. And even though they're competing for a starting position, they can still be friendly and learn something from each other. So I always tried to build some cohesiveness and avoid conflict. In my later years, when I had established a track record, I also spent a lot of extra time with younger players—sharing my experiences and giving them tips on how to play their position better.

I also find it interesting that baseball, while being a great team sport, is filled with many individual competitions. When you're a hitter standing up at the plate, for example, you're a soloist. It's you against the pitcher. No one else can help you at that moment. Your teammates can't help you. Your manager can't help you. And your dad can't help you. You have to execute on your own. For me, personally, when I was facing a great pitcher such as Roger Clemens or Nolan Ryan, I really savored the competition. I wanted to get a hit off those guys every time I faced them. It was a motivational force for me. "Okay," I'd think to myself before a game. "Roger Clemens is pitching today. This is going to be fun!"

I really believe that healthy competition is good in any organization. It tends to motivate people, drive them, focus their talent and energies. Most people agree that nearly every member of the team can be positively affected when energy is focused against another organization. Internal competition among employees, however, is a bit more controversial. Some executives say that employees should not compete with each other. I can understand that perspective. If not managed properly, internal competition can lead to territoriality, turf fights, fiefdoms, silos, and all those other business metaphors used to describe the same selfishness. On the other hand, when an organization has great leadership, internal competition can be motivating, synergistic, exciting, and fun. It can also lead to great success.

For such internal competitions to work, the first rule is that everybody has to realize that they're part of the same team. Trust and goodwill have to be established between people and departments. And to be effective over the long run, compensation and bonuses should be tied as much to team success as to individual results. I must admit that those internal competitions motivated me. And so did the bonus checks my teammates and I received when we made the play-offs.

In baseball, there is obvious competition against other teams. And I really enjoyed playing against great organizations such as the Yankees, the Tigers, the Red Sox, the Blue

Jays, and the Royals. As you might imagine, in a twenty-one-year career, rivalries came and went. But I will never forget the one that began in 1983 with the Chicago White Sox.

That year, the White Sox won the American League West Division. Manager Tony La Russa was in his first or second year with them. He was volatile, emotional, and protected his players at all costs. The Orioles won the American League East Division, which set up the 1983 Championship Series.

In the first game, Lamar Hoyt pitched a magnificent complete game for the White Sox. I got a broken-bat single in the ninth inning to drive in a run and make the final score 2–1. But it was really never that close. Hoyt was really in control the entire way.

In the second game, which we won, Mike Boddicker was our starting pitcher. He'd had a really good year for us, in part by throwing an unusual split-finger pitch called a foshball. It got its name by being a combination of a forkball and what we used to call a fish (a changeup). A fosh was a slow pitch that was hard to control. And that day, Boddicker had a few problems throwing it. As a team, our pitching staff only hit five batters all year. But in this game, we hit two batters. First, Boddicker hit Tom Paciorek with a curveball that slipped out of his hand. Then one of his foshballs popped Greg Luzinski, who simply let it hit him and then trotted down to first base. I wasn't really too worried about anything at this point, because I knew that the Baltimore Orioles pitching staff never threw at anybody. Earl Weaver had made it clear more than once that any pitcher who had to throw at somebody to get outs could find another place to play.

In the third game of the series, things really got interesting. Eddie Murray homered in the first inning to put us up 3–1. In the third, Mike Flanagan (our starting pitcher), tried to get a fastball by Ron Kittle on a 3-2 count. But the ball ran in low and hit him in the shin. You could tell by Kittle's reaction that it stung, and then he lost his cool and walked toward the mound. Of course, that caused both benches to clear. There was a lot of yelling, but no punches were thrown, and everybody quickly retreated to the dugouts.

When I came up to bat in the fourth, I asked the White Sox catcher, Carlton Fisk, why everybody was so upset. "We're not throwing at anybody intentionally," I said.

"Well, you hit five guys all year long," replied Fisk pointedly, "and now you've hit three guys in this series alone!"

"Oh!" was all I could manage to say. Now I understood that they thought we were throwing at them intentionally.

The first pitch to me from Rich Dotson was a breaking ball that bounced in the left-hander's batter's box. I knew this pitcher was good at hitting the outside corner, so I moved closer to the plate. The next pitch was thrown right at me and hit me in the butt. As I started toward first base, I remembered Fisk's remark and suddenly realized that I had been set up. The breaking ball was to make me lean out over the plate. And then somebody ordered a pitch thrown at me. I don't know if La Russa called it from the dugout, or if Fisk gave the signal on his own. Either way, it didn't matter. I was now angry, so I started screaming at Dotson.

Eddie Murray was the next batter and they threw at him, too. When the second pitch caused Eddie to jackknife, he pointed to the mound and started yelling at Dotson. Then the benches cleared and everybody was out on the field again. But the umpires managed to restore order before any punches were thrown, and things soon got back to normal.

When the game resumed, Eddie drew a walk, which put me in scoring position at second base. Sure enough, John Lowenstein stepped into the batter's box and ripped a double up the gap into right-center field. As I thundered around third base and headed toward home, I saw Carlton Fisk standing on top of the plate. I knew there was not going to be a play at home, and usually a catcher will stand away and let the runner score. But I was still mad about being intentionally hit, and I thought, "Well, if he doesn't move, I'm going to run him over." So I put my arms up to brace myself, and then, at the last split second, Carlton stepped forward. But he did it so late that my left arm clipped him on the way by—and he gave me a nasty look over his shoulder.

The next time I came up to bat, Carlton said, "I knew you were a hard-nosed player, Ripken, but I didn't think you were cheap." Well, that really made me angry and we started arguing and shouting at each other. Finally, the umpire stepped in between us and demanded that we get back to playing ball.

To make a long story short, we scored a lot of runs and won that game. And then we went on to win the series. But the message here is that I got so caught up in the competition, and so angry about what had happened, that I channeled all my energy into beating the White Sox. And that feeling lasted for years. Every time we played Chicago, all I had to do was look over at Tony La Russa or Carlton Fisk and I'd get mad. The most important thing in the world at that moment for me was to beat the White Sox. And I did hit unbelievably well against them. I probably batted .500 and hit more home runs and got more RBIs against them than any other team during that period.

After a while, Tony La Russa did a very smart thing. He waved the white flag and befriended me. It worked, too, because I lost my edge, and afterward I didn't hit any better against the White Sox than any other American League team.

COMMITMENT

During the summer of my junior year in high school, I was recruited to play with a small-town team called the Putty Hill Optimists. When Coach Marty Malloy offered me a position on his team, I immediately said yes. A week later, however, I regretted that decision when the best team in the city of Baltimore asked me to play for *them*. Johnny's (the city team) was a more elite, established team, and being a country boy from Aberdeen, I was extremely flattered. Not knowing what to do, I went to my dad for advice.

"What did you tell Mr. Malloy?" Dad asked.

"I told him I'd play for him."

"Then you will. You gave your word and you have to live up to it. You're committed to that program."

I was prepared to change my mind when a better opportunity came along. But my father made a simple statement that I had no trouble understanding. It was a very strong message that remained with me for the rest of my life.

There's not a doubt in my mind that commitment helped me persevere in breaking Lou Gehrig's record. During my career, I was committed to my organization, to my teammates, to my job, and to my profession. And those commitments spurred me on. In my mind, I had given my word to do the best I could do, and nothing ever changed that.

When I was first called up to play for the Baltimore Orioles, for instance, the public relations department asked me to participate in a lot of events. At first, I said yes to everything because I felt it was my duty to do so. But after a while, all the appearances started to wear on me. So, to concentrate more on baseball, I began cutting back on PR events. One of the first I turned down was a private gathering that was being put on by the Orioles' owner, Edward Bennett Williams. Within an hour, I received a phone call from Mr. Williams himself, asking me to reconsider. "Cal, I know you've been doing a lot for the team, and I really appreciate that," he said. "But I would consider it a personal favor if you would attend my event. It's really important to me."

Of course, I told Mr. Williams that I'd be there. But he did something at that event that I will never forget. As soon as I walked in the door, Mr. Williams came right up to me, shook my hand, thanked me for being there, and then personally introduced me to every person in the room. I had told Edward Bennett Williams that I would be at his event, and even though I was tired, I kept my word. And then Mr. Williams demonstrated his commitment to me by welcoming me personally and making sure that I knew everybody in the room. After that experience, I felt better about the Baltimore Orioles than ever. It was not only my dad's team, it was now officially my team. As a result, I had a new motivation to perform, and I didn't want to let anybody down.

I especially did not want to let down my teammates. Camaraderie on a good team is always tight. Once we earn each other's trust, we tend to count on each other when we're in the game. I certainly counted on my teammates. But the more overwhelming feeling for me was *my* commitment to *them*. They counted on me to be out there on the field, and I sure wasn't going to let them down.

In turn, each of us had a responsibility and a commitment to perform our specific jobs. A hitter in the middle of the lineup had to learn how to drive in runs. A hit-and-run guy was required to bunt and hit to the opposite field. A shortstop and second baseman had to work together to turn the double play in a variety of circumstances. A catcher had to work closely with his pitchers, and so on. Each of us had to come ready to play every game. It was our job, and that's what we got paid for. And personally, I always felt that if I was being paid to perform, then it was my duty to show up on time and do whatever the manager asked of me.

When the media started extolling his consecutive-games streak, Lou Gehrig expressed sincere surprise: "If a man earns his wages playing first base, isn't that where he is supposed to be? I belong on the ball field."

More than just my job, though, it was my profession that might have made me feel most committed. There is a beauty to baseball that, for me, makes it the greatest game in the world. It is America's pastime, with a strong history and tradition. All the great players, managers, and owners who came before me left legacies that should not be taken lightly. In my mind, those people were not to be let down.

I'll also never forget how my father looked when he put on his baseball uniform. He was transformed. A peace came over him that is hard to describe. I think the bottom line is that Dad was proud to be a member of the Baltimore Orioles and proud to be a part of baseball. He would never do anything to cast dishonor on either.

When I finally made it to the major leagues, that's exactly how I felt. I knew I was part of a great history, a great tradition, and a great sport.

When you're part of a great profession, it engenders pride in everything you do. And when you are proud of your profession, it's easy to go to work every day.

WHEN I ARRIVED IN BLUEFIELD, West Virginia, in 1978 for my first experience in professional baseball, I immediately realized that I was going to be the second-string shortstop. The starter at that position was Bob Bonner, a polished graduate of Texas A&M University. He had been a major college baseball player, was heavily scouted by the Orioles, and was four years older than I was.

The first time I took grounders next to Bob, I called home. "Dad, I'm never going to play," I said. "This guy is terrific."

"Hang in there and learn," Dad replied. "You'll get to play. That's what rookie ball is all about."

The organization soon moved Bonner up to AA, and all of a sudden, I had the opportunity to play every day, if I could earn it. In Bluefield, that meant two months' worth of games—a sixty-game schedule. During that time, as I was trying to adjust to the pros, I made thirty-two errors at shortstop, most of them throwing errors. I just couldn't get the ball consistently to first base.

In 1924, Lou Gehrig played in 134 games for the Yankees' minor league ball club in Hartford, Connecticut. That year, he committed twenty-three errors at first base.

I was really worried about how bad I was playing, too. Even though nobody said anything to me, I was certain that management was thinking that they should have started me out as a pitcher. But the truth was that, in rookie ball, we were all making mistakes. Few people at that level had the consistency of big league players. It was our responsibility to learn and improve as much as we could. So after the season was over, when I was invited to play in the instructional league, I went enthusiastically. While there, I really worked hard on improving my throws. I remember being fascinated at how

---

nearly all major league infielders threw the ball so it hit in the other player's chest—every single time. The ability to do that, I learned, comes from repetition, consistency, and experience. I worked so hard on this aspect of my game that, later in my career, I would become known for my throwing accuracy.

In 1979, I was promoted to A ball in the Florida State League. Shortly after the season started in Miami, our only third baseman was hit by a pitch and broke his wrist. All of a sudden, we had two shortstops and no third baseman. So the manager asked me to switch to third, which turned out to be a blessing in disguise. As I became more and more comfortable at third base, I remember thinking to myself, "Yeah, this is great. It's the same position that Brooks Robinson played."

As opposed to shortstop, third base seemed a more natural fit for me. Because I had more time to throw after I caught grounders, I stopped making so many throwing errors. At that stage of my career, things really clicked for me at third base. I think it may have been because I was still growing physically. At this time, I was six feet three and weighed about 195 pounds (as opposed to six feet two, 180 pounds, when I signed). By the time I made it to the majors, I would grow another inch and put on another thirty pounds.

After batting .303 in Miami and establishing myself as a solid third baseman, I was promoted to our AA team in Charlotte, North Carolina, for the 1980 season. The next year, the Orioles moved me to AAA ball in Rochester, New York—the last step before getting to the big leagues. That's where I caught up with Bob Bonner. Bob played shortstop, I played third, and we had a really good left side of the infield. Bob was still a great ballplayer. As a matter of fact, he had one of the best seasons at shortstop I'd ever witnessed. He was simply sensational.

That year, I started all 114 games, hit twenty-three home runs, and batted .288. But my most vivid memory of the season was the game I played on April 27, 1981. In my first at bat, I smashed a fastball over the left-field fence for a home run. The next time up, I hit a curve for another home run. And before walking up to the plate for the third time, I leaned over and told my manager that I was expecting the pitcher to throw me a slider this time. Sure enough, I guessed correctly and hit another home run. As I rounded the bases, my manager, Doc Edwards, jotted down a note to the Orioles' home office, which I was told about many years later. "Can't miss" was all it said.

EIGHT RIPKEN PRINCIPLES

---

2. A STRONG WILL TO SUCCEED

1. Turn a negative into a positive.
2. Channel your aggressiveness in a more productive direction.
3. Be willing to swing at a bad pitch. To succeed, you can't be afraid to fail.
4. You can only prepare so much. At some point, you have to test your plans.
5. Cheating your blind grandma at cards isn't fulfilling.
6. Healthy competition within any organization is good. It can be motivating, synergistic, exciting, and fun. It can also lead to great success.
7. When you give your word, you're committed. True commitment involves your organization, your teammates, your job, and your profession.
8. When your teammates are counting on you to be in the game, never, ever, let them down.

On May 3, 1982, I was mired in a terrible batting slump (batting only .121) when I stepped into the batter's box against Mike Moore of the Seattle Mariners. Mike was in his rookie year and really throwing hard. His 93–94 mph fastballs were striking out a lot of American League batters. In my first at bat against him, he crossed me up with a breaking ball, which I nubbed harmlessly back to the mound for an easy out. "Nobody gets me out with that little breaking ball," I muttered as I jogged back to the dugout.

A couple of innings later, as I stepped into the batter's box for the second time, I vowed to myself that I was going to hit Mike Moore's curve, no matter what. When his first pitch came in, I read breaking ball—not because it was *a breaking ball, but because I wanted it to be* one. *Well, this pitch was high and it started out coming right at me. So I waited for it to curve toward the plate. And I waited . . . and I waited . . . and I waited. Then suddenly, I realized that this pitch was not going to break. It was Mike's 94 mph heater and it was coming right at my head. I had stood my ground so long that all I had time to do was turn my head away, and then—BOOM!—the ball hit the back of my helmet and caromed into the air. I wound up flat on my back with a shattered helmet resting on the ground next to me.*

I must admit that Mike Moore really rang my bell. I was immediately taken to the hospital for all the standard X-rays and tests, which came back negative. But in a precautionary move, Earl Weaver kept me out of the lineup the next day. During that game, as I was sitting on the bench, I stewed about being hit in the head and became determined not to let pitchers get the best of me. If word spread around the league that I could be intimidated by high inside pitches, I would be picking myself up off the ground every time I batted. So it was important for me to make a stand, which I did.

Some people believe that whack in the head woke me up. And there's some truth to it, because I finally broke out of my rookie slump. I hit .281 the rest of the season.

In June 1934, the New York Yankees played an exhibition game against their minor league club in Norfolk, Virginia. Pitching for Norfolk was an up-and-coming fastballer named Ray White. In the first inning, Lou Gehrig smashed a home run off the young man. But the next time Lou stepped into the batter's box, White threw a fastball that hit Gehrig squarely on the crown of his head. As the ball caromed high into the air, Lou dropped to the ground, where he remained unconscious for about five minutes. (Note: This incident occurred twenty years before professional baseball players wore protective helmets.)

Lou was immediately taken to the local hospital for X-rays and diagnosed with a concussion. Yankee manager Joe McCarthy wanted to keep his star first baseman out of the lineup for the next day's game against the Washington Senators. But Gehrig insisted on playing. "I just had to prove myself right away," said Lou. "I wanted to make sure that big whack on my head hadn't made me gun-shy at the plate."

Borrowing one of Babe Ruth's caps because his own no longer fit due to the large bump on his head, Lou inserted himself into the lineup against the Senators and hit three consecutive triples—to left, right, and center. However, in the fifth inning, a torrential rainstorm washed out the game, and Lou Gehrig's three triples were not recorded in the record books.

CHAPTER 3

LOVE WHAT YOU DO

If I had to choose one thing that caused me to break Lou Gehrig's record,
it was the simple fact that I loved playing baseball. It's easy to go to
work day after day, month after month, year after year,
when you really love what you do. Every day is fun.
Every series is an adventure. Every game is important.

After I spent three years in the minor leagues, the Balti-more Orioles had to make a decision about me. They could leave me on the standard AAA roster, but another team would be able to draft me under Major League Baseball's Rule 5. Or the Orioles could put me on their forty-man team roster, which would signal their commitment to eventually bring me up to the majors. Such a move would also protect me from being selected by another club. Fortunately, at the end of the 1980 season, I was added to the forty-man roster and sent to Rochester to play for the AAA Red Wings.

I played well in the early part of the season, and when Doug DeCinces, the Orioles' starting third baseman, sustained an injury, there was talk of bringing me up right away. However, the Major League Players' Association had set a midsummer strike date, and upper management was fearful that if I was called up and then the strike happened, I'd be frozen in the majors and not be able to play ball. So they decided to let me stay in Rochester.

The looming strike dispute centered on the unresolved issue of free agent compensation. The owners had already lost at the bargaining table and in the courts, but were still adamant about receiving compensation for losing a player to free agency. Unfortunately, the strike did, in fact, go into effect on June 12, 1981, causing the cancellation of more than one-third of the season. By the end of July, a compromise was finally reached that gave the owners a limited victory by allowing a team that lost a free agent to draw from a pool of unprotected players. Part of the settlement for that year included the expansion of every team's major league roster by two slots. During the strike Doug DeCinces had plenty of time to heal from his injury, but there was still some question that he might not fully be recovered. So, on August 8, 1981, with the thought that I would be insurance in the event that Doug reinjured himself, I was given one of the new slots and promoted to the major leagues.

Two days later, during the twelfth inning of a game against Kansas City, I was sent in as a pinch runner for Ken Singleton, who had just hit a double. As I led off the base in my first big league game, second baseman Frank White called for a pickoff play. The pitcher wheeled and threw, but I got back in plenty of time. As Frank caught the ball and tagged me, he smiled. "Just checking, kid," he said. A few pitches later, the game ended when I scored the winning run.

On June 15, 1923, Lou Gehrig made his major league debut. In the ninth inning of a game against the St. Louis Browns (a team that would later become the Baltimore Orioles), Yankee manager Miller Huggins sent Lou in to play first base for starter Wally Pipp. The game ended when Lou fielded an easy grounder and stepped on first for the third out of the inning.

A few days later, in my first at bat in the majors, I hit a chopper over the mound off pitcher Paul Splittorf. From my view, it appeared the ball was going into center field. As I headed to first base happily thinking I had my first big league hit, I slowed up just a little to round the base. But Frank White came out of nowhere, backhanded the ball, jumped, and made an incredible throw to first to get me out by a fraction of a step. I went back to the dugout shaking my head and was greeted by my teammate Ken Singleton. "Welcome to the big leagues, kid," he quipped. "You've just been introduced to Frank White."

On June 18, 1923, Lou Gehrig got his first chance to hit in the major leagues. With the Yankees trailing by eight runs, Lou was sent in to hit for the pitcher. He struck out.

During the late innings of the next game, George Brett made it all the way to third base, and during a break in the action, we started chatting. "Haven't got your first hit yet, kid?"

"Nope," I replied.

"How many at bats?"

"Well, let's see. I'm oh for four today and was oh for four yesterday."

"Jeez!" Brett laughed. "You're oh for eight! C'mon, you can do better than that!"

I don't know why, but Brett's making light of the situation seemed to help me. And the next time I came to the plate, which was during a day game in Baltimore, I finally got my first hit. It was off Dennis Lamp of the Chicago White Sox. I hit a line drive in the hole; the shortstop, Bill Almon, dove and caught it on one hop, but he didn't have a play. They counted it as an infield hit.

On July 7, 1923, Miller Huggins sent Lou Gehrig in to pinch-hit for the pitcher in the ninth inning of a game against the St. Louis Browns. Lou smacked a line drive into right field for his first major league hit.

The following year, on May 31, 1982, I got my first stolen base in the big leagues. I always thought it was a curious thing, but I actually stole home. It was the front end of a double steal with Lenn Sakata on first and Al Bumbry at the plate. We put on a trick play where Len faked a move to second at the same time I took off for home. When the left-handed pitcher, Jon Matlock, whose back was to me, stepped off the mound to throw to first, he suddenly realized that I was heading home. But it was too late. I slid in under the tag in what was a close play.

> On June 24, 1925, Lou Gehrig got his first stolen base in the major leagues. He stole home on the front end of a double steal with Babe Ruth. Actually, Lou stole home fifteen times during his major league career.

I didn't have many starts during the 1981 strike season. But I did get to substitute every now and then for Doug DeCinces. The first few times I played third, veterans Jim Palmer and Mark Belanger both commented on my defensive play. "Ripken gets his hands out front so he can come up and in," said Belanger. "The last person I saw do that was Brooksie." Palmer was even more flattering when he said, "It's the second coming of Brooks Robinson."

To be compared to my boyhood hero by two guys who had played with him really made me feel great. But it didn't temper my frustration with not being in the game. The Orioles were in the hunt for the pennant, and DeCinces was all healed and playing very well. So for the remainder of the season, I just sat and watched.

I really hated sitting on the bench. And I vowed to myself that if I ever got in the lineup, I wasn't coming out.

PASSION

Most people think that, when I was a kid, my father drilled, trained, and generally force-fed baseball to me. But actually, he did the opposite. He planted a seed and tried to make it grow. Dad exposed me to baseball through his own love of the game. He enjoyed every minute of his career—and it showed whenever he threw a baseball, picked up a bat, or made out a lineup card. Baseball was fun for him. And as his son, I couldn't help but notice. When my father was having fun, I wanted to have fun with him.

By the time I was a teenager, though, Dad's message about choosing a career became more direct. "One of the problems today is that there are too many people working at jobs they absolutely hate," he would say. "The secret to happiness is not in the money you make. It's in the quality of your work and how it makes you feel. So find out what you love to do, pour yourself into it, and I'll support you along the way."

For me, there was never really any question about the career I wanted for myself. In fact, I never seriously considered any other options. I loved baseball. I loved it when I was a kid. And I loved it as an adult.

I thoroughly enjoyed going to the ballpark. I loved batting practice—being in the batting cage, swinging at the ball, the constant whir of the pitching machine. I loved taking infield grounders, working on double plays, throwing a thousand balls to first base. There was never a time clock to be punched. I'd show up early to the stadium and often be the last player to leave—sometimes long after the game was over. Then I'd get up and do it all over again the next day. When you play sports for a living, you never really have to grow up. And it's okay to act like a kid. For me, professional baseball made me feel as if I were twelve years old. I was playing a game. I was having fun. And there was nothing else I wanted to do.

Long after I retired from the major leagues, I realized that Dad's message to me was one of the most important of my life. If you find your passion, if you find something that you really love to do, then you never have to work a day in your life. To tell the truth, if I had to choose one thing that caused me to break Lou Gehrig's record, it was the simple fact that I loved playing baseball. It's easy to go to work day after day, month after month, year after year, when you really love what you do. Every day is fun. Every series is an adventure. Every game is important.

> *"This game is a continuous vacation for me."*
> **—LOU GEHRIG**

I remember one game that vividly illustrated how my passion for baseball kept me going. It was played on April 18, 1981, in Rhode Island between the Rochester Red Wings (my AAA minor league team) and the Pawtucket Red Sox and is now recorded as the longest professional baseball game in history.

We had a 1–0 lead after eight innings, but Pawtucket tied it up in the ninth, so we went into extra innings. The cold wind blowing in toward home made it difficult to score runs. In the bottom of the twelfth, a guy named Sam Bowen walked up to the plate and almost ended it. Sam was a strong, compact little guy who had a ton of home runs in AAA ball. But he never really made it to the big leagues. On a 3-0 pitch, he got a hold of a fastball and really cranked it. We all immediately thought the game was over. But as the ball sailed out toward the fence, the wind blew it back and our left fielder caught it right up against the wall. As Sam circled back from first base, he ran by our dugout and grinned. "Boys," he said, "if that ball didn't go out, we're going to be here a long time."

The truth of that statement resonated with us all as the game dragged on into the thirteenth, fourteenth, fifteenth, sixteenth, seventeenth, and eighteenth innings. Nobody scored. Between innings, the umpires and managers discussed whether there was a curfew in Pawtucket. They tried to call the league office, but couldn't get hold of anybody. And since nobody knew for sure if there was a time limit, we just kept playing.

It got so cold that night that we built fires in the dugout. We tore apart the bench and burned the wood to keep warm. A couple of guys who came out of the game in the ninth inning went into the clubhouse, had a few beers, and went to sleep. When they woke up hours later, they came out to the dugout and were shocked that there was no longer a bench and the game was still going on.

As the innings clicked by, those of us who were still in the game had to leave the warmth of the dugout to take the field. We were cold, tired, and wished somebody would just end this thing. "Oh, man," we said, "how long is this going to last?" "I don't care who wins." "What inning is it, anyway?"

We finally pushed across a run the top of the twenty-first inning. "All right," we thought, "the game's over. We've won it." But then Pawtucket scored a run in the bottom of the inning and the game went on. It was almost ridiculous.

After that inning, however, I noticed smiles on the faces of my teammates—and they grew bigger as each inning passed. We were now in uncharted territory. We wondered what was going to happen next. Pretty soon we got a little punchy, goofed around, and started to laugh. We were having fun again. And make no mistake about it, as time wore on, we really wanted to win that game.

Somebody finally got hold of the league president in the wee morning hours. "What are you guys still playing for?" he wanted to know. "The curfew was at midnight!" So the game was suspended at 4:07 A.M. We had played thirty-two innings in eight hours and seven minutes. The game would be picked up two months later in June, but it would last only one more inning. I got a hit but was stranded on base in the top of the thirty-third inning. Pawtucket scored in the bottom of the inning and won, 3–2. After the game was over, and the statistics were officially counted, my batting average dropped from .302 to somewhere in the .280s. During that one game, I had gone two for thirteen at the plate—a one-game batting slump.

But that's not the end of the story. After the game was suspended, some of us were so pumped up that we couldn't sleep. We were also hungry. Normally, for our after-game meal, my teammates and I met at the local diner for dinner.

This time, we found a twenty-four-hour Howard Johnson's and ate breakfast. As we talked about the game, we all realized that something special had happened. And the more we thought about it, the more proud we were to have been part of it all. We found out later that morning that we had just been in the longest professional baseball game in history—and I had played third base for the entire game. Wow!

Here's the kicker, though. Another game was scheduled that afternoon.

A lot of people who'd had that kind of day at work might not show up the next day. They might say to their boss, "I was up all night and I'm really tired. I don't think I'll come in to-day." And a lot of managers might agree. In general, it would be easy *not* to be at work the next day.

But I never even considered not showing up. I *wanted* to play that afternoon game. A lot of my teammates felt exactly the same way. We were proud of what we'd done, and we wanted to see what would happen next. After all, nobody had any inclination, when it began, that the previous night's game would be any different from any other.

After breakfast, I went back to the motel and slept for a few hours. Then I got up and went straight to the ballpark for batting practice. I think I was one of the first players to show up. It was love of baseball that brought me back. I *wanted* to be out there.

Awareness → Curiosity → Learning

When I was a teenager in high school, I read a quote in *Sports Illustrated* by baseball great Willie Stargell. "You get to the big leagues because you're talented," he said. "You stay there because you're smart."

I literally interpreted that as having to be intellectually smart to be a baseball player. So I made it a part of my master plan to concentrate on academics and keep my grades high. Of course, it wasn't until much later that I understood what Willie really meant. He was saying that it was a player's understanding of the details of the game of baseball that allowed for a long and successful career.

I believe that quote resonated with me, in part, because I had an innate curiosity about almost everything. I was a "why" kid. "I wonder *why* that happens?" "*Why* are we leaving now?" "*Why* is he doing that?" I probably drove my parents crazy at times, but I wanted to know everything—and I loved learning.

When I made it into professional baseball, at times I questioned why we were doing certain things. Dad had taught me how to play baseball the Oriole way. But when I got to Bluefield, some of the techniques the manager wanted us to use were clearly different. I was only eighteen years old, so I would get on the phone and explain the situation to my father. "You have to listen to what they say because they're in charge, Cal," my dad would say. "Always remember there is something you can learn from everyone. Try it their way, but remember how it's really supposed to be done." That's how I always tried to approach professional baseball. Nobody knows it all. You can learn something new every day.

The year I was called up to the majors, 1981, was Mark Belanger's final season with Baltimore. For seventeen years, he had been a rock at shortstop for the Orioles. He played next to Brooks Robinson and is considered one of the greatest defensive shortstops ever to play the game. From the moment I arrived, Mark took me under his wing. "You know, Cal," he said, "while you're sitting on the bench, you really need to look at the people who play the infield. Everybody tells you to watch the pitcher, but you can do both."

When we ventured to Detroit for my first series against the Tigers, Belanger made it a point to sit next to me on the bench. "Take a look at that kid at short," he said. "He's a pretty good guy to watch. He does things fundamentally right. He covers a lot of ground, he's fluid and graceful, and he makes very few errors. Now there's a player you could emulate." That shortstop's name was Alan Trammell.

I had grown up around baseball and I had spent three years in the minor leagues. But I must admit that when I got up to the majors, it was a whole new ball game. (Pardon the pun.) Virtually every aspect of the sport was performed at the highest level of execution and consistency. I had *a lot* to learn. And I knew that the quickest way to get sent back down to the minors was if I *did not* learn and adjust to this new level of competition. So I soaked up as much information as fast as I could.

I watched the infielders turn double plays. I noted how the fast runners stole bases. I studied how the pitchers threw to different batters. And after Ken Singleton took me down to the video room and showed me the replay of myself throwing a tantrum after striking out, I made it a point to watch how my teammate Eddie Murray reacted when he struck out.

He would always walk back to the dugout with his head held high, calmly put his bat and helmet back on the shelf, and take his seat on the bench. There was so much to learn—and so many good people from whom to learn. I welcomed advice and actively sought it.

A constant learner, Lou Gehrig often sought advice about how to be a better first baseman, and then took it to heart. "In the beginning, I used to make one terrible play a game," he said. "Then I got so I'd make one a week, and finally, I'd pull a bad one about once a month. Now, I'm trying to keep it down to one a season."

One of my greater skills as a baseball player, I believe, was my awareness. I was aware of the people around me, of what was happening in the game, and of the minute details that were occurring. I don't know if such a trait is genetic or if it's learned. I do know, however, that my parents always pointed things out to me when I was a kid, things that I wouldn't probably have taken much notice of otherwise. I remember when my dad and I used a hatchet and a string to trim the edges of the driveway. When we were finished and I was getting ready to walk away, Dad would stop me, put his arm around my shoulder, and say, "Look at that, Son. Doesn't that look great? Aren't you proud of your work?"

I believe that learning starts with awareness. When you're aware of something, you get curious. You want to dig deeper. You want answers. And when you're seeking out answers to your questions, you're learning. This simple process, *Awareness → Curiosity → Learning,* happened to me all the time when I was playing professional baseball. Let me give you just one example of hundreds I could have chosen.

As soon as I started playing shortstop, I began picking up pitches from the catcher to help me position myself. The type of pitch, its location, the count on the batter, and the batter himself dictated where I would play. When I saw the sign for an outside fastball and the count was 0–2 on Paul Molitor, for instance, I moved slightly more to my left in anticipation of where Molitor would hit the ball if he connected. Occasionally, however, the pitchers would throw a changeup without shaking off the fastball sign. Well, that would mess me up, because a changeup, being ten miles per hour slower, is more likely to be pulled by the batter and hit into the hole to my right. Once I became aware of this small thing, it made me curious about what was going on between the pitchers and catchers. So I went and talked to them. "Why do you guys do that?" I asked. "What's going on? Don't you know that you're crossing me up when a changeup is thrown on a fastball sign?" Then they informed me that the catchers and pitchers had an understanding that, if he wanted to, the pitcher was allowed to throw a changeup instead of a fastball without shaking off the original sign. "The pitch is just a little slower, Cal," they told me. "It doesn't really cause any problems for a catcher. We knew you were reading the signs, but we had no idea each pitch affected you so much."

I learned something new in that situation, and in the long run it helped me play better at shortstop. After that conversation, the pitchers began shaking off the fastball sign when they wanted to throw a changeup. *Awareness → Curiosity → Learning.*

I was also acutely aware that, at six feet four inches, I was an unusually big man to play shortstop. As a matter of fact, Earl Weaver took a lot of heat for moving me over to that position. Shortstops were supposed to be small, thin, wiry, and acrobatic. So I was very aware that I did not have the range to make those run-around backhanded plays like Ozzie Smith or Alan Trammell. The question for me, then, was "How do I compensate for that? How do I have success at this position?" So I started asking questions, seeking advice, and experimenting with different techniques. In the end, I realized that if I knew the hitting tendencies of every hitter who came up to the plate, and if I could see the signals the catcher was calling, then I could anticipate every hit ball and position myself accordingly. Basically, I just learned how to play my position better by solving a simple problem.

I carried that same problem-solving formula into business after I retired. Many people fail, I believe, because they are unaware of the core issue confronting them. They constantly run around putting out brush fires. But a lot of little fires take care of themselves if an executive focuses on the "one thing" that is causing all the problems. In essence, it's a matter of awareness. You have to be *aware* of the core problem. Then you have to be *curious* enough to find out what is going wrong. And finally, you have to *learn* from all the information you gather in order to come up with a solution. *Awareness → Curiosity → Learning.*

In general, I believe that continual learning goes hand in hand with success. And I'm certain that it helped me persevere in my consecutive-games streak. When I first reached the major leagues, I was like a young professional starting at a new company. I didn't know it all. I had to learn all the nuances of my job. I knew I had a huge learning curve and that it would take time for me to grow into the position.

Another lesson I realized very quickly is something that applies to all industries and organizations. The one thing that can knock you out of the lineup quicker than an injury is change. There are many threats to your job security. Some are internal. There could be a change of management. A more talented employee might come along and displace you. There are also external threats: a corporate buyout, an industry downsizing, a strike. Change is never-ending. But if you never stop learning, you can usually handle what comes along and adapt to the change.

After I reached the big leagues, Dad told me that, in order to have a long and prosperous career, I would have to "adjust and readjust." That's essentially the same thing Willie Stargell said. "You get to the big leagues because you're talented. You stay there because you're smart." Smart enough to learn and adjust, that is.

DEALING WITH ADVERSITY

In 1988, I was the starting shortstop in every game of the longest losing streak to begin a season. The previous year

(1987), my dad had been named manager of the Orioles. But lacking talent overall, we finished in last place. Going into 1988, we were in a rebuilding mode and our expectations were low. But nobody was prepared for what was about to happen.

We lost our first two games at home against the Brewers (0-2), and then journeyed to Cleveland and lost four straight (0-6). Back in Baltimore for a six-game home stand, I was informed that my father had been fired and Frank Robinson was coming down from the front office to take over. The team really went into disarray after that. Anything that could happen did happen. We lost all six home games against the Royals and Indians (0-12). Then we went back on the road and lost three at Milwaukee (0-15), three at Kansas City (0-18), and three at Minnesota (0-21).

In comparison to everything else that goes on in my life now, nothing will ever be as bad as what I refer to as "the old twenty-one." It was the worst possible situation to be in. Every time we lost, we received front-page headlines. Hundreds of fans sent us magic potions to help break the spell. We were receiving national recognition as the laughingstock of major league baseball. It almost made you numb. I wouldn't wish it on anyone.

During that losing streak, we had to cling to small threads of hope. We rearranged our goals, for instance. "From this point on, let's see how we match up." "Let's have a good month." "Let's have a good first half of the season." None of it worked.

The adversity, however, drew us together as a team. We became closer friends, better teammates, and helped support each other in little ways that we'd never done before. But as the losses mounted, so did the tension in the clubhouse. As everybody tried harder and harder to win, the hole we were in just got deeper and deeper.

Finally, after we lost our twentieth game in Minnesota, I couldn't stand it anymore. Late that night, while some of my teammates were moping around the clubhouse, I took a bunch of athletic socks and started wrapping them in tape. "What in the world are you doing, Rip?" asked one of the guys.

"I'm making tape balls," I said. "We're going to go back out on the field and play tape ball."

"What is tape ball?"

"You'll find out."

So four of five of us, including my brother Billy (who was playing second base for the Orioles), along with a bunch of the clubhouse boys, went back out onto the field. We threw down some makeshift bases, designated home plate as second base, and used a fungo bat to hit toward the backstop screen. Any ball hit into the seats was an automatic home run. Other than that, we kind of made up our own rules. For instance, as a pitcher, I would smash down the tape balls like saucers. They were flat on both sides, curved like Frisbees, and were difficult to hit. The kids called them saucer balls. It was so much fun. We played out on the Metrodome field until three o'clock in the morning. Emotionally, I can't tell you how much better it made me feel. And it turned out to be instrumental in changing my mind-set. I believe it helped some of my teammates, too, because, even though we lost the next game to the Twins, our mood in the clubhouse became a little bit brighter. And by the time we got to Chicago to play the White Sox, most of us had a new attitude.

In 1928, Lou Gehrig was playing stickball with a bunch of kids in the streets of his old neighborhood when he accidentally knocked a ball through the window of a local butcher shop. After he and all the kids were hauled down to the police station, Lou identified himself and promised to pay for a new window. The police sergeant let everybody go. He was a Yankee fan.

For some reason, I started thinking about a story my father used to tell to illustrate what a person is capable of when the chips are down. One afternoon, he saw a rat out in his work shed and chased it with a baseball bat. Dad finally cornered the rat, and having no place else to go, the rodent jumped up and attacked as if it were going to bite him in the throat. I guess his baseball instinct kicked in at that moment, because Dad swung and hit the rat with his bat. "At that moment, I just had to make contact," he told me. "And I did. It was like hitting a high and tight fastball."

Well, on April 29 in Chicago, I don't know what came over me, but every pitch that Jack McDowell threw was like that rat coming at my throat. I just had to make contact, and I did. I had three hits that night, including a home run. Eddie Murray also hit one out of the park, and we ended up winning the game 9–0 to end our twenty-one-game losing streak.

When I look back on the 1988 season, I sometimes feel the pain we all experienced. It's one thing to deal with something that goes wrong. But it's another thing altogether to deal with that level of adversity. After all, we almost didn't win a single game in the month of April (finished 1-22). Still, I'm thankful I endured that season. In the toughest of times, you can learn important lessons. And the most important thing I learned was that I could always fall back on the sport I loved to carry me through. That whole tape-ball episode was nothing more than a pickup game—a variation of baseball that reminded us we were supposed to be having fun out on the diamond. And when we combined that with a determination that we were better than 0-21, we snapped out of our depression and began to turn things around.

I never missed a game in 1988, even though it would have been easy to ask for a day off. We lost 107 games that year and finished dead last. But you know what? I was still playing baseball. And I loved it.

AFTER SITTING ON THE BENCH for most of my first two months of major league baseball in 1981, I went down to Puerto Rico to play winter ball. While there, I learned that the Orioles had traded Doug DeCinces to California. There was no question about it: Earl Weaver was counting on me to be his starting third baseman.

On Opening Day, 1982, I hit a home run in my first trip to the plate, went 3 for 5 overall, and was feeling pretty good about myself. Then I got only four hits in my next sixty-three at bats. All during that slump, I kept worrying that I was going to be sent back to the minors. Other players had been sent down for a lot less. But Earl Weaver believed in me and kept telling me so.

Earl was worried about only one thing. He was not convinced that I could hit outside pitches, because I stood a good distance away from the plate. So during batting practice one day, he stood behind the batting cage, told me to stand where I wanted to stand, then gave the go-ahead to my father to begin pitching, "Okay, let's hit!" he yelled.

Dad's first pitch was on the outside corner and I punched it to right field for a hit. His second pitch was also on the outside corner, and I punched it to right, too. When the third ball hit the outside corner, I knew it was a setup. Dad was a good batting-practice pitcher and I was well aware that he could, at will, throw the ball inside, outside, and down the middle. Clearly, Earl had told him to pitch me outside. So now I started to hit the ball hard. I bombed the next pitch over the center-field wall. Then I started pulling those outside pitches to left field, several of which left the park. After a few minutes, Earl looked at me and said, "Okay, so you *can* cover the outside part of the plate." And then he walked away.

Earl never did take me out of the lineup. He let me work myself out of that batting slump. But I really believe that, had I not been aware of what he and my father were up to and then started banging the balls to all parts of the field, Earl might have taken me out of the lineup for a few days or even sent me back to AAA ball to work on my hitting. As it was, I finally began hitting shortly after being beaned by Seattle's

75

Mike Moore on May 3. I'd been looking for a breaking ball but, instead, had taken a 94 mph fastball to the back of my head that shattered my helmet.

Near the end of the month, Earl had me sit out the second game of a doubleheader against the Toronto Blue Jays. Floyd Rayford started at third base for the Orioles. But then on May 30, 1982, I was back in the lineup—and I would not miss a game for the next sixteen years.

Baseball lore has it that Lou Gehrig's consecutive-game streak began when first baseman Wally Pipp complained of a headache and asked to sit out that day's game. For want of an aspirin, the legend goes, Lou was inserted into the lineup, and Pipp lost his starting job. It's a great story. But it really didn't happen that way. Gehrig's streak actually began on June 1, 1925, when manager Miller Huggins used Lou as a pinch hitter in the eighth inning of a game against the Washington Senators. Batting against Walter Johnson, Lou flied out to left field.

The next day, in the middle of a five-game losing streak, Huggins decided to scramble his lineup. He benched the first baseman (Pipp), the second baseman (Aaron Ward), and the catcher (Wally Schang). Finally given a chance to start, Lou played errorless ball in the field and went 3 for 5 at the plate (a double and two singles). The Yankees beat the Senators, 8–5, that day and snapped their losing streak. At the end of the season, New York traded Wally Pipp to Cincinnati. And Lou Gehrig did not miss a game for the next fourteen years.

EIGHT RIPKEN PRINCIPLES

3. LOVE WHAT YOU DO

1. The secret to happiness is not in the money you make. It's in the quality of your work and how it makes you feel.
2. It's easy to go to work day after day, month after month, year after year, when you really love what you do.
3. Always remember, you can learn something from everyone.
4. Learning starts with awareness. Then, when you're aware of something, you get curious. You want to dig deeper. You want answers. And when you're seeking answers to your questions, you're learning. *Awareness → Curiosity → Learning.*
5. The one thing that can knock you out of the lineup quicker than an injury is change.
6. If you never stop learning, you can usually handle what comes along and adapt to the change.
7. Adversity draws people closer together. You become closer friends, better teammates, and help support each other in little ways that might not have happened otherwise.
8. In the midst of adversity, to carry you through, you can always fall back on something you love.

Game number 444 of my streak occurred on April 10, 1985, the second game of the season. We were playing the Texas Rangers at Memorial Stadium in Baltimore. In the third inning, with me playing shortstop and Gary Ward the runner on second base, I looked at pitcher Mike Boddicker and put my finger to my eye. That was the signal for our version of the daylight pickoff play. I was going to sneak toward second, and if Mike saw daylight between the runner and me, he would turn and throw the ball to me.

I broke to the bag, Boddicker whirled and threw, and Ward dived back into second base. As I caught the ball, the spikes on my left shoe snagged on top of the base, and my ankle turned and rolled. I knew immediately this was worse than a normal sprain, because the pain was in-

stantly intense. After hobbling around for a moment or two, I threw the ball back to Boddicker and took my position at shortstop. (Gary Ward was safe on the play.) Between innings, our trainer taped up my ankle and I finished the game. X-rays taken afterward turned out negative. However, as soon as I removed the tape, my ankle ballooned up to twice its normal size. The doctor gave me a pair of crutches and told me not to put any weight on it.

As luck would have it, we were scheduled to play an exhibition game at the U.S. Naval Academy the next day. Rather than make the trip with the team, I stayed in Baltimore and received various treatments designed to reduce the swelling. Our next scheduled game was at eight o'clock the following night, which gave me almost two full days before I had to play again. In the meantime, the swelling lessened, if the pain did not.

Determined not to be knocked out of the lineup so early in the season, I taped up my ankle as tight as I could and started the game. As fate would have it, I was tested right away. In the seventh inning, I came to the plate with two outs, a man on third base, and the score tied. I hit a hard smash back at the pitcher, who got some leather on the ball, and it trickled behind the mound. Now I had to beat out an infield hit. Of course, it was my left ankle that made contact with first base, taking the full force of my weight with it. I was safe, the runner on third scored, and we ended up winning the game by one run.

Standing on first base, I remember thinking to myself, "Okay, my ankle hurts like heck. But it's got to get better from here on out." So I stayed in the lineup, and over the next couple of weeks, the pain in my ankle gradually disappeared.

CHAPTER 4

PREPARATION

I took it one day at a time and made sure I was always prepared.
Preparation makes you consistent. Consistency increases your value and
makes you irreplaceable. And then you're always in the game.

When I came to the ballpark on July 1, 1982, and checked the lineup posted on the bulletin board, I noticed the number 6 next to my name rather than the usual number 5. (In baseball, 6 designates shortstop and 5 third base.) I thought it was a mistake until Lenn Sakata, who had started at short the day before, came up and told me that I was, indeed, playing shortstop today.

Lenn had been battling with Bob Bonner for the starting position ever since the beginning of the season. But evidently, Earl Weaver wasn't totally happy with how it was going. (Bob Bonner never played as well in the major leagues as he did in the minors. Eventually, he left baseball to become a missionary in Zaire.) Meanwhile, I had come out of my early-season batting slump and had played in forty-four consecutive games without an error.

When Earl Weaver penciled me in at shortstop, he took a lot of heat from both the Orioles' front office and baseball traditionalists. After all, at six feet four inches, 225 pounds, I wasn't exactly the prototypical shortstop. In fact, Earl was intent on making me the tallest person ever to play the position regularly. When the media cornered him, Earl commented that I reminded him of a guy named Marty Marion, who played shortstop in the 1940s and 1950s with St. Louis. Marty, Earl pointed out, stood six feet two inches tall and had soft hands and played his position with grace. Earl also compared me to other shortstops in the league, saying, "It's too bad he's never going to play in an All-Star game. With Alan Trammell and Robin Yount in the American League, there's no way Cal will ever be selected." In retrospect, I find it amusing.

Just before the game began, perhaps a bit uneasy with his decision, Earl Weaver called me into his office. "Look, just make the routine plays," he said. "Don't try to go beyond yourself. If the ball is hit to you, make sure you catch it. Take it out of your glove, get a good grip on it, and make a good throw to first base."

I nodded and smiled as my manager spoke to me as if I were a Little Leaguer. But I think that was one of Earl's gifts. He usually spoke in a sincere tone and used simple words. As a result, people clearly understood the message he was trying to convey.

"If the runner is safe, at least he'll only be at first base," continued Earl. "But if you catch the ball and throw it over Murray's head, then not only will the runner be safe, he'll also be on second base. And we can't have that. Do you understand?"

"Yes, sir, I understand."

"Okay, then get out there and give us a good game."

When I took the field that day, I was under the impression that this stint at shortstop was only temporary. But it lasted fifteen years.

I completed the 1982 season with 93 RBIs, 28 home runs, and a .264 batting average. That was good enough to get me voted the American League Rookie of the Year. Other rookies that year included Kent Hrbek, Gary Gaetti, and Wade Boggs. The Orioles finished second in the American League East Division with a 94-68 record—only a single game behind Milwaukee. One of the greatest compliments I received in my career was Earl Weaver's postseason comment to the media: "I think if Cal had been at shortstop all year, we would have won the division."

As the 1983 season got started, people kept telling me I had to find a way to avoid the sophomore jinx. I'd made a big splash in '82 because the other teams had not yet figured out my weaknesses. This year would be different, I was told. The other teams would figure out how to pitch to me better, and in turn, I would have to make adjustments at the plate. All the Oriole veterans had seen it happen before. If I didn't adjust, they told me, I'd be in trouble.

My plan to avoid the sophomore jinx consisted of two things: awareness and preparation. First, I had to be aware of how the other teams were going to pitch me. I knew I did not have an overall weakness. I could hit fastballs, breaking balls, and pitches both inside and outside. When I recognized that the Yankees' strategy was to throw me breaking balls, for instance, I started looking for them. When it became apparent that the Red Sox were going to pitch me fastballs low and away, I moved closer to the plate and pounded them.

Of course, being aware of how the other teams were going to pitch me was only part of my plan. In order to break the sophomore jinx, I also had to be on top of my game. And the only way to do that was through extensive preparation. Once I knew the strategy a team was going to use against me, I would get to the ballpark early, take batting practice, and work on the types of pitches I thought they were going to throw that night.

On road trips, a lot of players would spend their free time sightseeing. But I never did much of that. Rather, I'd go to the stadium, put on my game face, and try to get psyched mentally. I was a serious ballplayer—not as relaxed as many of my teammates. Besides, a lot of the best times in baseball are in the preparation.

CONSISTENCY

During the middle of my career, I made only three errors in an entire season while playing every game at shortstop. And of all the things that happened during my career, those three errors remain in my memory as if etched in stone. Actually, I came very close to a perfect season.

My first error occurred relatively early in the season at Detroit. Cecil Fielder got jammed and punched a slow roller toward short. Because Cecil was a big guy who didn't run well, I had plenty of time to sneak up on the ball. The infield grass in Tiger Stadium is not the truest, and at the last minute the ball bounced up and hit me in the stomach. I smothered it, picked it up, and threw it to first base a little late. Runner safe. Error-6.

My second error didn't come until after I had played ninety-five straight errorless games, which was a record at the time. In Kansas City, I was playing George Brett to hit up the middle. But he got fooled by a pitch and cued the ball off the end of his bat, which sent it to my right. I had to run a long way to field that ball, and it was spinning away from me. The only real chance I had to make the play was to risk everything by taking a straight angle to the ball, backhanding it, then making up the time difference with the throw to first. A more conservative approach would have been to take a deeper angle to the ball, make sure I caught it, then hold it. In that case, the official scorer would rule it a hit. But I wanted to get the out. Unfortunately, when I tried it the risky way, the ball spun out of my glove. Runner safe. E-6.

The third error occurred in Milwaukee on a two-hopper hit in the hole to my right. I fielded the ball cleanly, but when I came up to make the throw, I noticed that our first baseman, Mickey Tettleton, was still moving toward the bag. Instead of throwing to first, as I should have done, I threw toward Mickey, who ended up having to come back off the base to catch the ball. The runner was safe. E-6.

There was a lot of media hype about my making only three errors all year long. After all, many shortstops can make three errors in a game, let alone the entire season. And, of course, I was questioned daily when I was in the middle of the consecutive errorless streak. Every time I went to a new city, I was asked the same things: "How do you do it?" "What's your secret?" "How can you be so consistent and error-free?"

The answers to these questions were complicated. First of all, I grew to love playing shortstop. It was a whole new world compared to third base. At third, I couldn't see the catcher's signs, so I never knew the logic behind pitch selection. When the ball was hit, about all I could really do was react. Of course, I was always searching for clues as to what the hitter might do. A little glance in my direction before the pitch, whether the catcher set up inside or outside, or stealing a sign from the third-base coach could all provide hints.

But when I got to shortstop, all the key information was sitting right in front of me and available to use. After a while, I got to the point where I could predict, with reasonable certainty, where the ball would be hit. And once I could do that, I increased my chances of getting outs by positioning myself in the proper place before each pitch. From that point on, making only three errors in a season came back to being consistent. Consistency comes from preparation, pure and simple. And mental preparation is just as important as physical preparation, perhaps more so.

Before every series with a new team began, our pitchers would meet with the catchers to discuss opposing hitters. They would go over advance scouting reports that would identify who was on a hot streak or who was in a slump. If a new kid had just been called up from the minors, there would be information about him as well. "He's hot. He went six for twelve in the last series. He's a pull hitter. He hit the ball to the left side eight out of ten times." Then, on game day, the starting pitcher and catcher would sit down with the pitching coach or the manager and come up with a specific plan on how to pitch to every batter.

Because all of the information that was being discussed in these meetings was useful and important to me, I inserted myself into the process. I would take extensive notes and study them before games. But as the season wore on, I relied on my memory to recall the strengths and weaknesses of hitters. How does this guy react to a 2-0 pitch? Does he yank it down the line? Is he a good fastball hitter? It was easy to remember, for instance, that when Reggie Jackson was in a slump, he tended to pull the ball on the ground. But when he was hot, he waited a little longer and, as a result, hit more shots to all fields.

I also had a fairly good memory for how hitters from the various teams matched up against our individual pitchers. Did they hit well or poorly against Mike Boddicker? Did they have a tendency to pull the ball against Dennis Martinez? Did they have trouble waiting on Scotty McGregor's changeup?

Where the pitches were to be thrown to each batter, and *what* that particular person's tendencies were (pull or opposite-field hitter), would clue me on whether he was more likely to hit the ball to the right or left side. Then I could position myself accordingly and increase my chances of getting an out.

This was all part of my mental preparation before games. But I also prepared physically. For example, thirty minutes before each game I jumped in the batting cage and got a good sweat going. And my batting routine rarely varied. First bunt the ball for timing—one down the first-base line, one down the third-base line. Then I'd imagine a hit-and-run play called with a guy on first base, so I'd hit behind the runner by smacking a ball to the right side. Next, I'd move the runner from second to third by hitting the ball to center or right field. And finally, I'd get the runner in from third with either a base hit or a sacrifice fly. This type of practice routine was important to me. It had been worked out over the years by various Oriole coaches, was a time-tested way to prepare players, and helped reduce the number of mental errors that might occur during games. In many ways, preparation *is* practice. And as Dad used to say, perfect practice makes perfect.

Early in his career, Lou Gehrig often committed mental errors while making a play at first base. "Every time I think," he said, "the ball club suffers." Determined to reduce his mistakes on the field, Lou consistently participated in practice routines designed to make him a better defensive first baseman.

Another routine that helped me immensely was pregame infield practice. When I played professional ball, it was almost ceremonial in nature, but few teams use it these days. Just prior to heading into the clubhouse, we'd all take our positions. After hitting four balls to each of the outfielders, one of the coaches would then hit the ball around to each infielder. First ground ball: Field it and throw to first. Then cover second base, take the throw from the catcher, and toss it around the horn. Second ground ball: Get two. Short to second to first. Take the throw from the catcher and toss it around the horn. Third ground ball: a bullet in the hole. Field it and throw to first. Fourth ground ball: slow roller, charge it, throw to first, then run up the tunnel.

In all the games during my streak, I don't remember missing a round of pregame infield practice. I needed those routines and thought of them as my last real test to make sure I was ready for the upcoming game.

I can point to one other element in my making only three errors in one year—and that was the glove I used. At the end of the previous season, I was in Minnesota when Kirby Puckett hit a hard grounder my way. The ball had so much topspin on it that, when it hit the hard part of my glove, it spun out. Kirby was safe at first base and I got an error on the play. That was *not* supposed to happen. I felt I had to try something different, so between innings, I picked up the more flimsy of my backup gloves and began using it instead. For some reason, that glove really worked. No matter where the ball was hit—whether it was a bad hop, an in-between hop, or

I didn't exactly catch it clean—if I got leather on the ball, it stuck in my mitt. I wound up using that glove all year long, and with each passing game, my confidence increased that I would catch virtually anything that came near me.

In general, I believe the ability to consistently perform with excellence is a result of both physical and mental preparation. I honed my skills by taking thousands of grounders and making thousands of throws to first base. With time, it became a matter of routine. Of course, the ability to make only three errors in an entire year did not happen overnight. I'll never forget committing thirty-two errors in my first season of minor league ball. But eventually, I gained control of my body, and with enough repetition, I was able to garner both consistency and confidence. In addition, by joining the pitcher-catcher meetings, I was able to gain access to information and, as a result, was able to perform my job with more precision.

Since my retirement, I've noticed that many people in business do not seek access to critical information. Rather than interact with people from whom they might be able to glean an advantage, they tend to remain in their own little worlds. But gaining access to key, up-to-date, and reliable information is an important part of preparation. In turn, proper preparation helps you create a better game plan. It *increases* your chance of success and *decreases* the risk that something will go wrong. Consistency comes from preparation.

PERSONAL ACCOUNTABILITY

During my three-error season, I closely analyzed each of the errors right after they occurred. The Cecil Fielder grounder called for caution. It called for plenty of time. I don't know if I could have anticipated the bad hop. Maybe if I'd picked it up a little crisper, instead of fumbling for it, I could have thrown him out. I've caught bad hops before, every shortstop has. Or maybe it wasn't my fault after all. Perhaps I should have blamed the infield at Tiger Stadium. It's always been a minefield out there.

On the George Brett play, I really believe the only chance I had to get him out was to take the risk and go for it. But could I have done something slightly different to make that play? What about moving my glove out a little farther? No, I don't think so. Maybe, after the game, I should have gone in and argued with the official scorer. Maybe it was his fault.

And what happened with Mickey Tettleton? I got surprised that he wasn't yet at first base. But maybe I could have waited a moment for him to get there. Maybe I could have thrown the ball at the bag, rather than straight at him. On the other hand, if Mickey played first base more often, he would have gotten there faster. Was it his fault?

In the end, I couldn't blame the infield at Tiger Stadium. I knew it was unpredictable. I didn't blame the official scorer. I knew the risk involved when I decided to go for that ball in the hole. And I wouldn't blame Mickey Tettleton. He was my teammate. It wasn't the infield, it wasn't the official scorer, and it wasn't my teammate. It was me. I made those errors.

And I had to learn from them, because each of those situations would probably crop up again.

Regardless of the profession in which you're engaged, you can usually find somebody to blame for your failures. In baseball, it's particularly easy to locate a villain. All you have to do is look for the guys dressed in blue. I always thought the umpires had particularly difficult jobs. When they were good at what they did, nobody said a thing. But when they made a mistake, or did anything that was the least bit controversial, *somebody* would be in their faces on the field or screaming at them from the stands.

I'm fairly proud that, during my major league career, I was only ejected from three games. Given my natural competitive tendencies, I find that to be one of my most amazing statistics. But I did really work hard at staying in the game when my temper got the best of me.

The first time I got tossed was on September 25, 1987, six years into my career. Tim Welke was the umpire behind the plate that day. Our careers paralleled somewhat, and he had seen me evolve from a hotheaded kid in the minor leagues who threw temper tantrums and helmets. When I stepped up to the plate, I watched as the first pitch, which was way out of the strike zone, was called a strike. Next, I swung at a ball and fouled it straight back. Then I was called out on a bad pitch. As I turned and walked away, I just could not hold my tongue. "You missed two out of the three strikes," I sarcastically said to Welke, without looking at him, "and the only one you didn't miss, I swung at."

Well, that must have made him mad, because he quickly

started following me back toward the dugout. When I heard him coming, I stopped. But he was already so close to me that, when I turned around, the tip of my helmet made contact with his mask. It was totally accidental, but Welke got angry and shouted, "You're out of the game!"

"What?" I asked. "Why did you throw me out of the game?"

The ump really had no answer for me. I think he had reacted impulsively and couldn't take it back. So I was out of the game and that was that.

On June 14, 1933, Lou Gehrig got into a heated discussion with the field umpires over whether Boston Red Sox runner Rick Ferrell had run out of the baseline between first and second base. The argument escalated when the Yankee manager, Joe McCarthy, charged out of the dugout and entered the fray. In the end, both Gehrig and McCarthy were ejected. It was one of only six times that Lou was thrown out of a game.

Two years later, I probably deserved to be thrown out of a game. It happened in the bottom of the first inning of a home game against Minnesota. Roy Smith was pitching for the Twins that day, and I thought it would be a comfortable at bat because he did not have overpowering stuff. Rather, Roy was a control pitcher who nibbled at the outside corners.

Our first two batters, Mike Devereaux and Phil Bradley, were called out on strikes. Both shook their heads in disgust as they walked away. The umpire, Drew Coble, was clearly giving Smith a wide strike zone and it was working against us. So, as I approached the plate, I felt that if Drew was calling a wide strike zone that night, it was my responsibility to make him aware of it.

The first pitch to me was just a little off the outside corner. I took it for a strike, but felt it was close enough that I couldn't really argue about it. The next pitch, however, was about a foot outside. Strike two. Now looking down at the dirt and moving my cleats around, I decided to say something. Usually, umpires will appreciate the fact that, by not looking directly at them, the fans will not know an argument is going on. "Drew, that first pitch was close, a bit outside," I said. "But the second pitch was way outside. Somehow, you need to take a better look."

Just as I got my toehold in the batter's box, Coble stepped right up behind me and shouted, "You guys are always complaining!"

When he came into my space, it changed the tone of the argument. "Well, more than just you knows what a strike is," I said.

In response to that, the ump said something that I felt was really unwarranted, and I took offense to it. "Look, I was just trying to give you a message, and you escalated this whole thing by coming out from behind the plate," I said. "Why don't you just get out of my face."

"Why don't you get out of *my* face?"

Well, that really made me mad and I just lost it. "You brought your big, fat butt out from behind home plate and you put your face in my face," I screamed. "Now you're telling me to get out of your face. You know what, you're a dumb SOB."

"You can't call me that!" he screamed back. "You're outta here."

In the end, I had to be carted off the field by my teammates. That was the angriest I had been on a baseball field in a long time. It was a bad scene, and I did not handle the situation well.

I felt even worse, however, when I was later told that a man and his young son had saved their money and driven up from Virginia just to see me play. They had great seats in the second row, and right before their eyes, I got thrown out of the game in the first inning without even having taken a swing. Well, it just ruined their day and the youngster cried for the entire game. Fortunately, a season-ticket holder offered up his seats for the next day's game.

It was bad enough that I had lost my cool and been ejected from the game. But it was another thing, altogether, to have affected that youngster's day so negatively. The entire situation really ate at me, and I relived it over and over again. Perhaps I could just have turned to the umpire and said, "Okay, that's enough. I've said what I wanted to say and I'm going to hit now." Maybe if I'd just had the wherewithal to do that, it might have ended right there. As it was, that incident stuck with me for the longest time, and afterward I worked hard to control myself better in the heat of competition.

During that period of introspection, I remember asking myself more than once if outside forces affected my ability to behave and perform well, if I was dependent on them. I finally answered that question during an autumn game in

Toronto, when a drainage problem caused water to leak in between the flooring and the artificial turf. Overnight, the water froze and created a buckle in the turf right around my normal position at shortstop. When I got out on the field, I had to make a decision—either gripe at the groundskeeper, complain to the umpires, or make the best of it. I decided to gut it up, play in front of the hill, and take the problem completely out of the picture. I would not allow myself to be dependent on outside forces. I would be dependent on myself. No excuses. No complaints. Just work with what you have and do the best you can.

I believe that, over the long haul, holding yourself personally accountable helps you succeed—whether it's in baseball, business, or life. If it's always somebody else's fault, you end up never solving your problems. But if you focus on your own performance, rather than blaming outside forces or other people for your failures, you have a chance to get better.

At the end of the day, I think it's all about looking yourself in the mirror. And personally, I could never lie to myself.

INCREASING YOUR VALUE

If I was going to play ball every single day, I had to be deserving to be in the lineup. But in baseball, you can't always get the game-winning hit or make the game-saving catch. Those big things only happen once in a while. It's the little things that tend to define your value to the team. "If you take care of all the little things," Dad once told me, "you never have one big thing to worry about."

During my career, I was always trying to contribute to the team any way I could. That included intangible things such as bunting a runner into scoring position, driving in a run with a ground ball, turning a double play at a key moment, or executing well on a cutoff or relay play. The more ways I could find to contribute to the team, I felt, the more valuable I would be to the manager.

> Lou Gehrig was always looking for ways to contribute. He noticed, for instance, that the right-field wall in Yankee Stadium was slanted to the right, and whenever a ball was hit out there, runners would try to advance to second or third, depending on Babe Ruth's ability to field the ball. So Lou would cross the middle of the infield and back up second or third base. Back then it was rare for a first baseman leave his position in such a manner.

Let me give you an example of one intangible that most fans were completely unaware of.

Early in my career, I began building good relationships with Oriole pitchers and catchers by asking them about their strategies in throwing to different batters. After one such discussion, a young pitcher in our organization, Storm Davis, who was due to pitch against the Red Sox the next day, actually asked me for advice. "I just don't know what to do with these hitters," he said. "Got any suggestions?"

"Let me think about it," I replied. "I'll write up a plan for the Red Sox hitters and give it to you tomorrow."

"Okay," he said. "I'd be grateful for any help."

That night, I went back to the hotel and jotted down my suggestions on a yellow pad of paper. "First hitter, Wade Boggs. Very patient at the plate. Almost always takes the first pitch. Throw your first pitch right down the middle. Second pitch on the outside edge (he'll probably foul it off). Still a great hitter on the 0-2 count, though. Fastball on inside edge for strike three. Next batter, Marty Barrett. Likes to do this. Jim Rice, a good hitter. Will make you pay for mistakes over the middle of the plate. Pitch him inside until he proves he can hit your fastball. Then throw curves and changeups."

I did that for every hitter in Boston's lineup, and the next morning I gave Storm my scouting report. He read it, thanked me, and put in his pocket. That night, he went out and dominated the entire Red Sox batting order. Storm's success really built up my confidence, and as a result, I worked even harder to study the opposition's hitting.

By the time the 1990s rolled around, I had established a great rapport and a good reputation with most of the Oriole pitching staff. One of our most talented young pitchers was Ben McDonald. He threw hard and had all kinds of stuff, but he always seemed to be snakebitten by the big inning. During one tense situation, he was having a conference at the mound with catcher Chris Hoiles. I thought it was taking a little long, so I ran up to find out what was going on. "Well, we're just talking about how to pitch out of this jam," said Ben.

"Mind if I offer some advice?" I asked.

"Please do, Cal."

"Well, this guy is an early fastball hitter. Throw him a curveball, strike one. Another curveball, strike two. Then he becomes more flat-footed. Finish him off with a fastball on the inside edge."

Sure enough, Ben struck out the batter on exactly the three pitches I had recommended. Afterward, he began looking to me in key situations. I would always accommodate him, but after a while, it got to be a bit too much. "Look, Ben," I finally said, "I can't run up to the mound every time you want me to help with pitch selection. So I tell you what. I'll develop a sign I can flash to the catcher if you need a suggestion." Both Ben and Chris agreed to the arrangement, so periodically I would help out while I was still at my position. Well, sure enough, the three of us clicked, and Ben went on a winning streak.

Right about this time, Scott Erickson came to Baltimore in a trade with Minnesota. "I don't know Scott at all," Chris said to me. "And with the White Sox, we're up against a pretty tough lineup. Do you have any ideas?"

"Well, I've been hitting against Scotty for a while," I responded. "He's basically got two great pitches—a nasty, heavy sinker ball and a sharp slider. But he's always had trouble getting these guys out, because they have left-handed hitters who dive into the plate to go for his outside sinker balls."

So I started sending signals to Hoiles behind the plate. In turn, he flashed them to Erickson, who was more than willing to throw whatever his catcher wanted. During that first game, I called for a lot of inside fastballs. Sure enough, Scotty threw a great game and we won in a blowout. Afterward, he was happy. "Wow! I've never had success against the White Sox," he said. Of course, I didn't tell Scotty I was calling the signals from short. I let Chris take the credit.

We continued that way for a while until one day when Hoiles got knocked out of the lineup after being hit by a foul tip while he was batting. Backup catcher Gregg Zaun was called in from the bullpen and started scrambling to get ready. That's when I pulled him aside. "Look, Zauny," I said, "I've been helping Hoiles with pitch selection. Would you like me to give you that same set of signs?"

"Yeah, it would help a lot."

"Okay, here's what I do. The left side of my body means the pitch goes to the left side of the plate. Right side of my body, right side of the plate. My ears mean fastball. My nose, curveball. Chin, slider. Belt, changeup. And if I flare the front of my glove with my right hand, that means forkball. Got it?"

As we were confirming the signals, Scott Erickson walked by and saw us. "What's going on?" he asked.

"Zauny's coming in to catch," I said. "Every once in a while, when he gets stuck on the signals, I'll flash a sign to help."

"Oh, okay."

As the game progressed, Scotty was dominating the hitters. But then, just before the seventh inning started, he came over to me. "Are you still calling some pitches?" he asked.

"Yeah, I make a suggestion every once in a while."

"Well, stop it, will you? I want to work on some breaking balls."

"Sure thing," I replied.

———

From that point on, I stopped calling the signals, and unfortunately, Scotty went into the tank.

Before long, I was calling signs for quite a few members of our pitching staff. But, for a variety of reasons, that turned out to be a touchy subject. Some of the coaches might have thought I was going over my boundaries as a player. Another problem was that it was risky. If the opposing team recognized what I was doing, their batters would know what was coming. In the end, however, the risk was worth the reward—especially from my point of view. I may have been helping the pitchers and catchers, but I was also helping myself. I had advance knowledge of the pitch and could therefore set up my defensive positioning earlier. In turn, that would give me a better chance of covering my ground and also decrease my chances of making an error.

I remember one time when Paul Molitor came to the plate when Ben McDonald was pitching. We got ahead in the count, 0-2, and I called for one of Ben's 95 mph fastballs on the outside edge of the plate. At that point, I was 100 percent sure that Ben was going to hit his spot. And I was 100 percent sure that Molitor, if he made contact, would not hit the ball to the left side of the infield. So I moved way over, stood near second base, and played him to hit it up the middle. Sure enough, that's exactly where the ball was hit.

I can still hear Molitor after I threw him out at first base. "How the hell can you play me way over there!" he screamed in frustration.

"It's easy," I muttered to myself. "I'm calling the pitches."

That's just one example of my trying to find more ways to

contribute to the team. Of course, the more ways you can contribute, the more you increase your value. If the manager was thinking about taking me out of the lineup for some reason, and it was on a day that Ben McDonald was pitching and Chris Hoiles was catching, I'm relatively sure that one or both of them would have said something about it.

From the beginning of my career, I was determined to keep my destiny in my own hands as much as possible. If the manger had to make a tough decision about me, I wanted him to sit in his office and agonize over it. If I was in a batting slump, I wanted him to think something like "Well, I may be able to replace his bat, but if I take him out, what about all the other things I'll be losing? What about his fielding? What about his leadership on the field? The hub of the wheel might collapse and we'd fall apart. Nope, he has to stay in. It would just create too big a hole to fill."

Of course, I had to count on my boss's knowing all the little things I did to help the team. But at the major league level, any manager who didn't realize what was going on wouldn't last long. So I never really worried about it.

My overall philosophy was pretty basic. Before every game, I asked myself, "What can I do to help us win this particular day?" I took it one day at a time and made sure I was always prepared. Preparation makes you consistent. Consistency increases your value and makes you irreplaceable. And then you're always in the game.

. . .

IN OCTOBER 1983, I played in my first World Series. I was twenty-three years old and nervous as all get-out. As I took the field, I was worried about the whole world watching. Then that first ground ball was hit to shortstop. I fielded it cleanly and threw it over to first base for the out. Going back to my position, I remember exactly what I was thinking: "That's the same ground ball I got for 162 games during the regular season. Same ball field. Same ground ball. Same throw. What am I worried about?" You can't prepare for what it's going to feel like to be in your first World Series. But you can prepare for all the plays you're going to make during the World Series.

That year, we beat the Philadelphia Phillies in five games. I was fortunate enough to record the final out of the Series when Garry Maddox hit a humpback liner right at me, and I caught it. What a thrill. And what a terrific team we had. An infield that included Eddie Murray, Rich Dauer, Ken Singleton, Rick Dempsey, and Todd Cruz. A starting outfield of John Lowenstein, Al Bumbry, and John Shelby. And a pitching staff that included Scott McGregor, Mike Boddicker, Storm Davis, Mike Flanagan, and Tippy Martinez. World champion teams like ours just don't come along very often. I was proud to be part of that group.

The 1927 World Series champion New York Yankees had one of the greatest teams in baseball history. Known for their late-inning home runs that sportswriters referred to as "five o'clock lightning," the heart of the Yankee lineup included Babe Ruth, Lou Gehrig, Earle Combs, Tony Lazzeri, Bob Meusel, Mark Koenig, Joe Dugan, Pat Collins, and pitchers Waite Hoyt, Herb Pennock, Wilcy Moore, and Urban Shocker. Collectively, the team was known as Murderer's Row.

Nineteen eighty-three was also a good year for me personally. I led the majors with 211 hits and 47 doubles, was second in both extra-base hits (76) and total bases (343), and finished with a .318 batting average. In the field I led the American League in assists, chances without errors, and double plays—with a final fielding average of .970. A month after the Series ended, I was voted Most Valuable Player in the American League—barely edging out my friend and teammate Eddie Murray. That made me the first player to win Rookie of the Year and MVP in back-to-back seasons. *So much for the sophomore jinx!* I didn't realize it at the time, but I also played in every inning of every game in 1983.

In 1927, Babe Ruth hit 60 home runs, had 164 RBIs, and batted .356. But Lou Gehrig won the Most Valuable Player Award in the American League. That year, Lou batted .373, belted 47 home runs, and set a major league record with 175 RBIs.

On May 6, 1984, I hit for the cycle (single, double, triple, and home run) in a game against the Texas Rangers. It was the only time I accomplished the feat. The only other Baltimore player ever to have done that was Brooks Robinson.

Lou Gehrig hit for the cycle twice. The first time was on June 25, 1934, in a game against the Chicago White Sox. The second was on August 1, 1937, against the St. Louis Browns.

On May 4, 1985, after I'd played a game in Minnesota, a reporter came up to me and asked if I knew what I had just done. "What are you talking about?" I asked.

"Well, you just passed Brooks Robinson's record for consecutive games by a Baltimore Oriole. He had 463. Today, you played in number 464."

"Really?" I responded. "No kidding?"

In June 1933, a reporter came up to Lou Gehrig and asked him if he knew how many consecutive games he had played. "No, I don't," Lou replied. "I guess it must be up in the hundreds somewhere."

"You've played in 1,250 games in a row," said the reporter. "At that rate, you'll break Everett Scott's major league record this season."

"Gosh, I had no idea," replied Lou.

EIGHT RIPKEN PRINCIPLES

4. PREPARATION

1. The ability to perform consistently with excellence is a result of both physical and mental preparation.

2. Interact with people from whom you might be able to glean an advantage. Gain access to key, up-to-date, and reliable information.

3. Proper preparation helps you create a better game plan. It increases your chance of success and decreases the risk that something will go wrong.

4. If it's always somebody else's fault, you end up never solving your problems. But if you focus on your own performance, rather than blaming outside forces or other people for your failures, you have a chance to get better.

5. If you take care of all the little things, you never have one big thing to worry about.

6. The more ways you find to contribute to the team, the more valuable you will be to the manager.

7. Keep your destiny in your own hands as much as possible.

8. Before every game, ask yourself, "What can I do to help us win this particular day?"

During a game against the Seattle Mariners in the mid-1980s, I hit a pitch into the left-field corner for what looked like an easy double. But the left fielder got to the ball quickly and made it a close play at second base. When I saw the throw coming in, I realized the second baseman was catching it blind (meaning he didn't know exactly where I was). The ball got to second ahead of me, but it was a little off-line, and as the second baseman reached around to make the tag, I slid safely away from him. During that slide, however, I braced myself awkwardly and hyperextended my elbow. At first, the pain really bothered me. But I shook it off and stayed in the game.

When I came to the on-deck circle for my next at bat, I gingerly swung the bat to test my elbow. "Ouch, that really hurts," I said out loud without thinking.

"You all right, Rip?" asked one of my teammates in the dugout.

"Yeah, yeah. I'm okay," I said.

But when I swung the bat harder, it hurt a little worse. Even though I kept my mouth shut this time, I was thinking I might not be able to hit. "Well, there's only one way to test it," I thought. So I stepped into the batter's box.

The first pitch to me was a fastball, low and away, on the outside corner. When I swung and missed, the pain was so intense, it brought tears to my eyes. I stepped out of the box to regroup, then got back in there. I hit the next fastball on the nose to the second baseman, who threw me out at first. As I headed back to the dugout, I suddenly realized that my elbow did not hurt when I hit that ball. "Hmmm, contact doesn't hurt," I thought, "but swinging and missing does."

Rather than taking myself out of the game in order to let my elbow heal, I decided to use the injury to make me a better hitter. "If I was going to swing the bat," I reasoned, "it was just going to have to be a meaningful swing. I had to get a good pitch to hit." Of course, that was the secret to being a good hitter, anyway. So I decided to be more selective each time I went to the plate.

Sure enough, I started hitting like gangbusters. During the next week, I think I got fifteen hits in my next twenty-five at bats. I was more patient, more disciplined, and I really focused on trying to anticipate exactly what the pitcher was going to throw. The more successful I was, the more positive and optimistic I became.

The pain in my elbow persisted, and it would sting when I swung and missed a pitch or tried to make an awkward throw from shortstop. My arm didn't totally heal until I was able to rest it for a couple of months after the season was over.

CHAPTER 5

ANTICIPATION

*The beauty of baseball is that, even when you lose one, there's an
optimism about the next day. My father used to say it all the time,
"Keep your chin up, kid. There's another game tomorrow."*

Very early in my major league career, Earl Weaver pulled
me aside for some batting advice. "This pitcher is nib-
bling the outside corner," he said. "So when the count is two
and oh, why don't you sneak up on the plate during his
windup? Then that outside pitch will be right in your power."
I tried out Earl's advice later in the game and ended up pulling
the ball over the left-field fence for a homer.

After that experience, I stepped up my efforts to anticipate
pitches and adjust accordingly. But rather than moving during
the windup, I'd set my position prior to the pitch's being de-
livered, based on the pitcher and the likelihood of a certain
pitch coming in. For instance, in order to have a better chance

at hitting a knuckleball before it fell out of the strike zone, I'd move up in the batter's box. After a certain amount of success, I gained a reputation as a hitter who had a pretty good knack for anticipating pitches. Some people thought I was just guessing. But I viewed it as a combination of common sense and learning from experience. After all, if I got a base hit on a fastball my first time up against a certain pitcher, during my second at bat I could safely look for a different pitch—a slider or, perhaps, a curve, depending on that particular pitcher's strength. Sooner or later in that at bat, I'd get it.

While most people realized I anticipated pitches as a batter, I don't think it was generally recognized that I also anticipated pitches while in the field. Here's an interesting example. In 1993, Harold Reynolds came over to the Orioles after playing second base for a decade with the Seattle Mariners. During the last five of those years, he combined with shortstop Omar Vizquel as one of the most effective double-play combinations in baseball.

Harold and I got together in spring training and talked about how we were going to work together. One of the most important elements we had to get clear involved who would cover second base on throws from the catcher or pitcher. We agreed that I would make the call from short. I would hold my glove over my face and look at him. A closed mouth (lips together mouthing the word "me") would signal that I would cover. An open mouth (mouthing the word "you"), and it would be his bag.

During the game, when a runner reached first base, I looked over at Harold, signaled, and he shook his head that he understood. Before the second pitch, however, when the situation changed, I tried to give him a different signal, but he wasn't looking at me. "Hey, Harold," I yelled. "You have to look at me before every pitch. The signal might change."

"Well, Omar and I used to signal only once, when the hitter first came up," he replied.

"No, it changes. A pull hitter might not be a pull hitter on an oh-and-two fastball on the outside corner. I need you to look at me before every pitch."

It took Harold a while to adjust to that new routine because, after all, he'd spent most of his career doing it a different way. But it didn't take long for him to be convinced that it was the right thing to do. During one of our spring training games, with a runner on first base, a right-handed hitter stepped into the box. Normally, Harold would cover the bag, but I suspected a hit-and-run play where the batter would wait on the pitch and try to hit the ball behind the runner. In that case, Harold would have to be in position to field a ground ball and throw the guy out at first. Otherwise, if he covered second to take a throw from the catcher, the batted ball would go through Harold's vacated position, and we'd be looking at runners on first and third.

So, before the pitch, I gave him the open mouth, which signaled that I would cover. Well, Harold's eyes got big, indicating that he had expected to cover second. Sure enough, the runner was stealing on the next pitch, the batter punched the ball right at Harold, and he threw to first base for the out. "How did you know?" he asked me with a big grin on his face. "How did you know the batter was a hit-and-run guy?"

"Well, I didn't know," I replied. "But I knew the runner was not a base stealer. So if he ran, chances are that it would be on an orchestrated play, a hit-and-run." Harold was really impressed with my system, and he wanted to learn as much as he could about it. Eventually, I opened up a whole new world to him.

REDUCING YOUR RISK

"Do you always try to throw the hitter out by a half step?" an umpire once asked me.

"I'll take what the runner gives me," was my response.

With that question, I got the impression that some umpires felt I was making their job more difficult by adjusting my play at shortstop in order to make it a close play at first. Of course, I didn't do that on purpose. I was simply utilizing all my options.

Many shortstops treat every grounder and throw to first base in exactly the same manner. But to me, there were many variables that could change how I handled a play. The individual hitter was one of the most important factors. If he was a fast runner, I had to be quick in fielding the ball and making the throw. A slow runner would give me more time. The type of ball hit also impacted my approach. If it was a slow roller, I'd have to charge the ball to gain enough time to throw out the runner. A hard-hit grounder, however, and I could take my time. There was no need to hurry the throw. Doing so would only increase my chances of making an error.

With experience, I was able to develop a series of checkpoints that helped me gauge how much time I was going to have on every grounder. As soon as the ball left the bat, for example, I'd use my peripheral vision to note whether the runner slipped in the batter's box, didn't run hard, or got a fast break toward first. In general, I took whatever time the runner gave me.

Sometimes, because all situations aren't equal, there was a decision to make after I caught the ball. With a guy on first base, all grounders are not double-play balls. If the base runner is particularly fast and got a good jump on the pitch, I might have to throw to first to keep out of a big inning. Or if the batter hits me a three-hopper, and he runs fast, my play might be to take my time, make sure I catch the ball, and then get the out at second base.

In general, I treated every player, every situation, every inning, and even every pitch differently. Many shortstops would not take these variables into account on a straight ground ball. They viewed it as the same play. But I saw it in a hundred different ways. For me, it was a matter of controlling the situation to reduce my risk of making an error or not getting an out.

Now that I'm retired, I basically do the same thing. I treat every person, every opportunity, and every deal as a separate and distinct entity. With experience, I've found that a cookie-cutter approach is simply not an effective way of conducting my affairs. Because individuals like the personalized treatment and the customized structure of a deal, they are more likely to work with me. In business, as in baseball, treating everything uniquely reduces risk and, as a result, increases the chances for success. And, of course, the more successful a person is, the more likely it is that he'll be penciled into the lineup.

Over the years, I also came to realize that a general approach to risk reduction helped my chances of not receiving a serious injury. In that regard, I was never afraid to send a message when I felt it was appropriate. Every baseball player knows, for instance, that one of the quickest ways to get knocked out of lineup is by being hit with a pitched ball. The number of players who have had their careers ended or been seriously injured is troubling to contemplate. So whenever I felt I might be in danger, I took some sort of action.

A few years before Lou Gehrig retired, the career of Detroit catcher Mickey Cochrane was tragically cut short after Yankee pitcher Bump Hadley hit him on the left temple. Lou himself was hit in the head three times. One time, he was knocked unconscious and had to go to the hospital. The two other times, he recovered and stayed in the game.

During a game in Baltimore, for example, Cleveland pitcher Dennis Martinez drilled me in the small of the back with a fastball. I knew he didn't do it intentionally. I think he was trying to pitch me inside and the ball just got away from him. Still, I was left with a very painful bruised back, and I did not want that to happen again. Dennis was an old teammate of mine who had been traded years before, so I knew him well. After this particular game, he came into our weight room to use the facilities, which was a courtesy the Orioles provided to visiting teams. When I saw Dennis, who, at five feet eleven inches, 185 pounds, is much smaller than me, I immediately went over and picked him up in a playful bear hug. But as I was doing it, I jammed my knuckle into the small of his back in the exact position where his pitch had hit me. "Cal! Cal!" he started yelping. "That hurts! That hurts!"

So I let him go and said, "Okay, now you get the picture, Dennis. That's how it felt when you hit me in the back today." The next time I went to Cleveland and stepped into the batter's box against Dennis Martinez, the first pitch was about a foot outside. And if I remember correctly, Dennis pitched me away for the rest of my career. He never came close to hitting me again.

That incident occurred about halfway through my career. In 1983, the year I was voted MVP, I remember being terribly intimidated by New York Yankees, right-handed pitcher Goose Gossage, who threw a 100 mph fastball. After a game against the Yanks in Baltimore, I heard my teammate Tim Stoddard call up Gossage (who was an old friend) and suggest that they get together with some friends at a place that was only five minutes from my house. Well, I dropped by after the game, and when Tim saw me, he invited me to join the group. That evening, I spent two or three hours socializing and found out that Goose Gossage was a great guy. And I think he liked me, too. From that point forward, I was never intimidated by Goose, and he never threw a pitch that came anywhere near hitting me. As a matter of fact, I found myself feeling unusually optimistic when I stepped into the batter's box against him.

OPTIMISM

During the 1983 season, on our way to winning the World Series, we endured two eight-game losing streaks. During one of
them, Orioles owner Edward Bennett Williams came down
to the locker room and tried to pump us up. They way he did
it, however, was unusually impressive, especially for a twenty-
three-year-old kid like me.

A trial lawyer by profession, Mr. Williams walked around and
spoke to each of us, individually, as if we were members of a
jury. When he got to me, he said, "You know, Cal, we both have
jobs that are right out in front of the public, where everybody
can judge us. So we each have to figure out how to work in that
context. If I lose a case, I'm done for. But in your 162-game season, you can fail sixty times and still have an excellent year."

I had never before thought of an entire baseball season in
such an optimistic light. It not only motivated me for the remainder of 1983, but it resonated with me throughout my career. Mr. Williams's comment seemed to fit my personality,
which I always believed was naturally optimistic. And when I
really began to think about it, so did my chosen profession of
baseball. At the plate, all you have to do is get three hits in ten
at bats to be considered a great hitter. So even though you fail
70 percent of the time, there's still reason to be optimistic.
And that keeps you keep coming back.

I suppose it's possible to win every game in a six-month-
long baseball season. But it really isn't very realistic to think
you'll go undefeated. Actually, no team has ever been able to

do it. I think it's a given that you're going to lose at least sixty games, even if you're an excellent team. Part of the beauty of baseball is that, even when you lose one, there's an optimism about the next day. My father used to say all the time, "Keep your chin up, kid. There's another game tomorrow."

I also believe that baseball helped temper my hatred of losing, which, of course, led to a lot of bad behavior when I was young. I learned early on that losing is not only part of baseball, it's part of life. Great learning takes place through experience. Sometimes, it's good to lose. Sometimes, you need to feel the pain before you can do better the next time out.

Throughout my career, I met a lot of people who always seemed to be upbeat. Take Terry Crowley, the Orioles' hitting coach, for instance. A big part of Terry's success was due to his unfailingly optimistic personality. He spent a lot of time with us in the batting cages, and his optimism couldn't help but rub off. Actually, I believe he spent just as much time trying to get us into a positive frame of mind as he did working on where we held our bats. "Best swing of the day!" was his favorite expression. "You're doing really well."

> **Lou Gehrig** was a fairly optimistic person, even in the face of being diagnosed with amyotrophic lateral sclerosis, a terribly debilitating disease. **"I believe that I will be well on the way to recovery very shortly,"** he wrote in a letter six months after the initial diagnosis. Sadly, it wasn't to be.

After I retired and began working in business full-time, the optimism of Steve Bisciotti (owner of the Baltimore Ravens) also inspired me. Steve's early career was spent in sales, and he used to tell a story that sounded more as if it were coming from a baseball player then a businessman. "I could be zero for ten or eleven in the morning session of sales calls," he would say, "and I'd be the happiest person in the world. Why? Because I knew the law of averages would make my afternoon session great!"

Optimism comes naturally to people like Terry Crowley and Steve Bisciotti. But it doesn't come so easy for others. Some people are pessimistic most of the time. I've even run into a few who are doom-and-gloom almost every day. Over the years, I noticed that a pessimistic attitude actually helped some of my teammates. Their fears, worries, and anxieties motivated them to perform. It never worked for me, though. Through the course of a season, in which I had to deal with all kinds of changes and different situations, dwelling on negatives just sapped my energy and prevented me from performing well.

I always felt that the best way to move forward was with a positive frame of mind. If I had a miserable day, rather than moping around, I tended to be honest with myself. I'd evaluate the situation and formulate a plan based on what I knew I *could* do. All my preparation, all my "perfect" practices, all those grounders and throws, all those hours in the batting cages, gave me the confidence that I had skills I could count on. And once I focused on those skills, I was able to dig deep down to pull myself out of a batting slump or a mental rut.

I'm certain that having an optimistic frame of mind helped me persevere and play in 2,632 consecutive games. Of course the streak wasn't all rosy. The first 1,000 games or so didn't receive a lot of notice. I think it kind of snuck up on everybody. And when it got to 2,000 games, most people focused on the excitement of my passing Lou Gehrig. Between 1,000 and 1,500 games, however, there was a great deal of negativity, in part, because the media took notice when I passed Joe Sewell, Billy Williams, Steve Garvey, and Everett Scott.

The Orioles were also going through a rebuilding process back then. There was a lot of turnover, and as a team we weren't very good. As far as I was concerned, the streak shouldn't have come into the picture at all. But it did. The media jumped all over me: "Cal's being selfish. He needs to step aside for the good of the team." "Ripken cares more about the streak then he does about his teammates." Too much stuff like that started to get to me. At one point, I recall thinking back to the 1986 All-Star game and a conversation I had with Dale Murphy of the Atlanta Braves. Dale had voluntarily ended his 740-game streak the week before because he got tired of dealing with the pressure. But he urged me *not* to sit down for the same reason. Later, somebody also told me about how Billy Williams (Chicago Cubs) ended his streak in 1970 after 1,117 consecutive games. All the media pressure started to sap his energy, and as the story goes, he hit a ball at Wrigley Field that had triple written all over it. But he settled for a double. Upset with himself, he went to his manager, Leo Durocher, and asked for a day off.

During that rough period of negativity associated with our

rebuilding, I had also seen my teammate Eddie Murray attacked mercilessly by the press. Eddie was one of the best switch-hitters in baseball history, a future Hall of Famer, and a wonderful human being. But all that didn't matter. The club wasn't doing well, Eddie was our leader, and people started pointing fingers at him and blaming him for all our troubles. The truth is that it was no more his fault than anybody else's. But the negative momentum gathered until he was traded away by upper management. It broke my heart.

Eventually, I realized I was going to have to deal with the media onslaught, because all the negativity began to drag me down. But how was I going to manage the problem? Should I stay out of the public spotlight, speak only to Oriole management, and trust in them? Well, that didn't exactly work for Eddie. In the end, I decided to go on TV and radio to speak directly with the public. "Look, we're in a rebuilding phase," I would say. "I know we're not winning a lot of games. I'm as frustrated as anybody in the stands. But I'm an Oriole. I'm in it for the long haul. And I'm going to work twice as hard to fix it." I never knew for sure whether that made much of a difference with the fans, team ownership, or the media. But it sure helped me deal with the negativity. I was able to get back into the proper frame of mind, which, in turn, helped me stay in the game.

As the streak progressed, my experiences (both good and bad) built on one another. I learned, for example, that when I was mired in a batting slump, the law of averages would eventually catch up to me. I also knew deep down inside that I was not a .200 hitter. So rather than dwelling on the miserable, I remained optimistic. Conversely, I was also realistic when I was on a hitting streak. Just because I was hitting .400 or .500 didn't mean it was going to stay that way. I knew things were going to drop off again. So I rode the wave while it was up and tried not to get too depressed when I came back to reality. And many times, I found that success would come when I least expected it. Just because I had a fever, for example, didn't mean I wasn't going to do well. Remember that time when I hyperextended my elbow, then went on a hitting streak? It could happen again.

When you're optimistic, you become empowered. When you're empowered, you're more likely to be successful. And when you're successful, you almost always are proud of what you've achieved.

Every individual should define his or her own success. For me, it was being appreciated by my teammates.

I remember one particularly difficult situation in a game at Yankee Stadium. We were in the field, the Yanks had runners on first and second, there were no outs, and the score was tied. I could see that my teammates were worried. A few of them had that "deer in the headlights" stare. So I called time and pulled everybody together on the pitcher's mound. "Hey, guys, we know they're going to bunt," I said. "This is no different than any other time we've been in this situation. If worse comes to worse, we make sure we get the out at first. Then we concentrate on the next batter. C'mon, let's go! We can get out of this!" We survived that inning and later won the ball game. Afterward, one of my teammates said my pep talk made all the difference.

Moments like these are the greatest. Optimism is hope. Hope makes everybody feel good. It leads to self-worth and confidence. It makes everybody believe "Yeah! We can do this!"

CREATING ROADS OF OPPORTUNITY

A lot of people think I made a smooth transition from baseball to business. For the most part, they're correct. But the reason it went smooth is because I planned for the end at the beginning.

When I first made it to the major leagues, a number of veterans were preparing to retire. Jim Palmer, Al Bumbry, and Ken Singleton, among others. The money was starting to get good, but it was still not enough to guarantee financial security. I guess curiosity got the best of me, because I really wondered what they were going to do now.

"Do you have any regrets?" I asked many of the veterans.

Some of their answers stuck with me: "I wish I had planned more." "I wish I had taken the thought of retirement more seriously." "I wish I would have played in more games while I had the chance."

When Lou was just getting started in major league baseball, he went to his manager, Miller Huggins, for advice. Huggins encouraged him to start planning for his retirement right away, rather than waiting until it was too late. Heeding that advice,

Lou invested in Florida real estate and learned the ins and outs of the stock market. As a result, he had few financial worries when it came time to retire.

These guys were at the end of their careers. I was at the beginning of mine. So, determined to learn from them, I created a plan that would give me options when I did finally retire. First, I sat down with my agent and tried to convince him that I could do more than simple endorsement deals. I was marketable and I wanted to be more proactive. It took a while, but I finally persuaded him that it would be in both our best interests to expand my business opportunities. Five years later, I formed a service company designed to take advantage of the money I was earning and the people I was meeting. Along the way, we started going down a path that I didn't particularly like. So I brought it back to my fundamental goal of staying involved with baseball and working with children.

After Lou Gehrig retired, he spent as much time as he could with children. "I've always been interested in kids and young fellows," he said. "I've been talking to them and their dads for years at father-son banquets and such. Maybe now, I'll be able to say the right word at the right time to fellows who need it most."

With time, the business built upon itself, and toward the end of my career, some exciting things happened. A kids' baseball league was named after me. I got going on a fantastic sports complex for kids in Aberdeen, Maryland, my hometown. All of a sudden, the road I had plowed at the beginning of my career was yielding all kinds of opportunities.

By the time I did actually retire, I didn't have time to sit around and mope that I was no longer playing major league baseball. I had jumped into my business so completely that, when spring training rolled around, I barely noticed. I'd carved out future for myself, I had plenty to do, I was having fun—and I owed it all to a little bit of long-term planning.

There's a great irony in baseball, as there is in life. You execute on the short term. You play day to day, and as the saying goes, you can't play tomorrow's game until it gets here. But without a great deal of effort, you can prepare for the future. The choices you make early on regarding your investments, the people with whom you associate, where you live, and virtually every other aspect of your future can pay huge dividends down the road.

Of course, it also helps to have people around you who think the same way. My first big league manager, Earl Weaver, was a long-term thinker. Actually, I sometimes wonder what might have become of me if it hadn't been for Earl. In 1982, I went 4-64 at the plate for the month of April. That's an .062 batting average! I lot of other managers would have sent me back down to the minors without blinking an eye. And no one would have blamed them. But Earl kept saying, "No, he's going to be all right. He's going to make it."

As a young ballplayer, I used to think people made their

own opportunities. If you were good enough, you could make your own breaks. Nobody could hold you down. I still believe that, to a degree. But with time, I learned that the organization for which you work also holds your future in its hands. For instance, I noticed that the Orioles sometimes designated young people as their future prospects. But if you weren't on the list, you could end up rotting in the minor leagues. Well, I wanted to be one of those future prospects. And I made sure I was considered by doing everything I could think of that would make upper management believe I was the caliber of player they were looking for.

When I was in the minor leagues, I accepted invitations to participate in the instructional league during my first two off-seasons. My willingness to play extra baseball (in order to develop faster) was not shared by some players, who felt the season was too long as it was, and that they should let their bodies rest. But look at what happened during my two stints in the instructional league. The first year, I went as a short-stop and the other guy at that position didn't show up. So I was able to improve my skills by playing every day. The next year, I went in as a third baseman. But the second third base-man had to have surgery due to an injury. So I was able to play every day once again. In the 1980–1981 off-season, I went down to Puerto Rico to play winter ball. While there, I played third base. Originally, I had intended to play shortstop. But when I asked manager Ray Miller why he wasn't playing me there, he cryptically replied, "Don't worry about it, kid," which perplexed me a bit. Still, I was in the mix with a lot of other big league ballplayers, and that summer I contended for the Triple Crown (league leader in batting average, home runs, and runs batted in).

In the long run, I really believe that my desire to play in the off-season not only improved my skills but earned me the respect of my managers and coaches. When they looked at me and saw that I had done really well, I believe it convinced them that I could be the Orioles' future starting third baseman. As a matter of fact, toward the end of the season in Puerto Rico, I was informed that they had traded Doug DeCinces, which sealed the deal. Of course, that's what Ray Miller was referring to when he told me not to worry about playing shortstop. He already knew that DeCinces was going to be traded and that I would be called up.

My desire to play every day, coupled with my willingness to play wherever I was needed, opened up another door that I never expected to walk through. When Earl Weaver penciled a 6 next to my name instead of a 5, he never said a word to me beforehand. I think that was due, in part, to Earl's knowing I was open-minded enough to give it a shot if that's what he wanted.

When he got around to having that talk with me, I could have said that I didn't want to make the switch: "I'm a third baseman. I was told I was going to be a third baseman. I feel comfortable there. That's what I want to do." I *could* have said all those things, but I didn't. The truth is I was happy to give it a try, and at any time I would have considered changing again if asked. And when I got to shortstop, I liked it. Not only did I do well there, the rest of the team started to play better. So I stayed at shortstop for the next fifteen years—until I was asked by my manager to move to third base.

FROM JUNE 5, 1982, to September 14, 1987, a span of five years, I played every inning of more than nine hundred straight games. My string of 8,243 consecutive innings was thought by some to be a major league record, even though nobody had ever kept the stats before.

It all ended in the eighth inning of an 18–3 loss at the hands of the Toronto Blue Jays. Interestingly enough, it was my dad (manager of the Orioles at the time) who pulled the plug. In the top of the eighth, Dad plopped himself down on the bench next to me and asked, "What do you think about coming out?"

I paused a moment, then responded, "Well, what do you think?"

"I think it would be the right thing."

"Okay, then."

And that was it. But when our guys took the field in the bottom of the eighth without me, I didn't feel good about myself. There had been a lot of media talk about my being tired, both mentally and physically, from never missing an inning. Because I didn't believe all that stuff, I felt I was abandoning my ideals by sitting down. My brother Billy (playing second base for us) said that when he saw the look on my face, he knew it would be a long time before I again missed playing every inning of a game. As I settled down on the bench, Larry Sheets tried to cheer me up. "Hey, Rip," he said. "If you ever want to know what to do on the bench, just let me know. I can provide plenty of advice."

After Lou Gehrig ended his consecutive-game streak and took a seat on the bench, pitcher Lefty Gomez tried to make him feel a little better. "Just think, Lou," he said, "it took fifteen years to get you out of there. I'm out sometimes in fifteen minutes."

I was only on the bench for twenty minutes. But it was a *very long* twenty minutes. And the truth is that I felt lost.

When I returned to the hotel that night, I sat down and wrote out all my feelings on about a dozen pieces of stationery. It was past three o'clock in the morning when I got to the final page. "I have no feeling of anger, regret, or disappointment," I wrote. "I also have no feeling of relief. I take tremendous pride in my ability to play every day, but I don't believe it to be a great accomplishment. The innings thing seemed to go hand in hand with the games streak. I do, however, have strong feelings about continuing the games streak."

On the day after my dad pulled me out of the lineup, my brother Billy ripped all the ligaments in his ankle. He was out for the year.

Eight years later, I would break Lou Gehrig's record.

EIGHT RIPKEN PRINCIPLES

5. ANTICIPATION

1. All situations aren't equal. Treat every person, every opportunity, and every deal as a separate and distinct entity. A cookie-cutter approach is simply ineffective.

2. When you feel some sort of pending danger, don't be afraid to send a message if you think it's appropriate.

3. It's possible to win every game, but it just isn't very realistic to think you'll go undefeated.

4. Even if you're zero for ten in the morning, the law of averages can make your afternoon great.

5. The best way to move forward is with a positive frame of mind.

6. Define your own success. Plan for the end at the beginning. But remember, you can't play tomorrow's game until it gets here.

7. Even though you execute in the short term, you can, without a great deal of effort, prepare for the future.

8. A desire to work every day, coupled with a willingness to do whatever is needed, can open up doors that you would, otherwise, never expect to walk through.

In the first half of 1990, I experienced a terrible batting slump. At one point, I had gone 14 for 82, and by June my average was barely above .200. I tried to avoid looking at the scoreboard because I couldn't bear seeing that low number up in lights. And for one of the few times in my career, the fans in Baltimore booed me.

The slump actually carried over from the previous September when we were in the middle of a pennant race. I was the only proven hitter left from the 1983 championship team, and opposing teams were concentrating hard on how they pitched to me. As a matter of fact, several pitchers told me they would get fined if they let me beat them. I tried to be patient, but I wanted to contribute so much to help our team win the division that, after a while, I began swinging at bad pitches. That was a terrible mistake—thinking I could extend the strike zone and have any degree of success. By early 1990, the only thing keeping me in the lineup was the fact that I was having my best year in the field. That was the year I only made three errors and finished with a major league record .996 fielding average.

So there I was—thirty years old, an eight-year veteran, and struggling badly. I wondered whether my skills were starting to deteriorate, and how long I could last as a big leaguer. I thought about asking my father for help, but at this point I had outgrown his level of experience. It was not that I'd lost confidence in him, but I just needed the advice of somebody with more experience who understood what I was going through. That's when my manager, Frank Robinson, stepped forward. One of the greatest hitters in baseball history, Frank was not only a Hall of Famer, but a true student of the game. His level of experience was just what I needed.

"Let's talk, Cal," said Frank, as he called me into his office and shut the door. "You know I had a long career. At one point, I felt like I'd never get a hit again. In Cincinnati, they described me as 'an old thirty.' And when they traded me to Baltimore the following year, I used that remark to motivate myself—and I won the Triple Crown."

Frank didn't pressure me, he offered his advice. I immediately accepted and we went down to the batting cages. "You seem to be having trouble controlling your forward motion," Frank said. "You're excitable, wanting to charge at the pitch. Why don't you spread your stance and go into a bit of a crouch. That will anchor you to the ground more and control the lunging." Frank also suggested that I stop the constant movement of my bat. He had me rest it on my shoulder until the pitcher began his windup. Then I lifted it into the hitting position.

I'll always be grateful to Frank Robinson for taking an interest in me when I needed it most. He actually restored hope in my swing. And the result was remarkable. I batted .278 the rest of the season to raise my final average to .250. Then I worked hard in the off-season on all the things Frank and I had practiced.

Over the last twenty-two games of the 1927 season, Lou Gehrig (a lifetime .340 hitter), batted only .275 with a measly nine extra-base hits. He also committed fourteen errors during that span.

Miller Huggins would have let Lou sit out the final game of the season. After all, the Yanks had already clinched the pennant, the crowd was sparse, and the game was essentially meaningless. But rather than take a game off and rest for the World Series, Lou stayed in the lineup. On that day, he hit his forty-seventh home run of the year.

"A good hitter will always remain a good hitter," said Gehrig. "Good batters, like good salesmen, hit slumps. All will pull out of them if they keep hustling."

In 1927, the New York Yankees not only won the World Series, but Lou Gehrig was voted the American League's Most Valuable Player.

CHAPTER 6

TRUSTING
RELATIONSHIPS

I don't think you can be successful in anything without the help, friendship,
and goodwill of other people. Your teammates and colleagues rely on you,
and you rely on them. More than anything else in the world,
I wanted to be counted on by my teammates to be in the
lineup every day.

"Rick, I'm really bothered," I said to my teammate pitcher Rick Sutcliffe. "This whole streak thing. I don't know if it's good or not. All the pressure is driving me crazy, and I'm considering taking a day off. But I know if I do, there will be a big media blitz. I'll have to deal with it in the short term, but maybe things will then get back to normal. What do you think, Rick?"

We were on the field at Cleveland's old ballpark, Municipal Stadium. It was obviously a period of doubt for me. The team wasn't doing well. I wasn't playing particularly well. And I was again catching a lot of flak for being selfish and not taking myself out of the lineup.

After a moment's pause, Rick looked at me rather seriously. "Well, I'm pitching tomorrow," he said. "And if you take a day off *tomorrow*, I guarantee you'll make the papers. You'll be in the front pages. You'll be in the sports sections. You might even make the business sections. But there's one more section you'll be in."

"What's that?" I asked.

"The obituaries—because I'm going to kill you." Rick Sutcliffe outweighed me and, at six feet seven, stood three inches taller. When he made that remark, he did not have a smile on his face. And I'm sure I looked at him a little bit troubled.

"Cal, you've had it right all these years," Rick continued. "I'm a starting pitcher. I only get to play one out of every five days. When it's my turn to pitch, I want the very best lineup behind me so it gives me a chance to win. The other four starting pitchers feel exactly the same way. You do so much more for our team than hit and field. You bring stability to the infield, you bring the right decisions, and we want you behind us.

"Right now, you're in a bit of a slump. All you have to do is go fix your hitting. I don't know. Do what you normally do. Learn how to bunt for a couple of games or something. But stop your whining and go back to your job."

That was all I needed to hear. By being straight with me, Rick Sutcliffe snapped me out of my funk. And from that point on, I never doubted myself or varied my approach again.

TEAMMATES

Nearly every year I played professional baseball, there was a challenge to my starting position. The old-school way of handling that kind of test was to be territorial. Don't give the other guy a chance. Don't talk to him. And above all, don't be nice to him.

I just couldn't do it that way. Even the smallest bit of common sense made me realize that the other player on the field was my teammate. Just because we were being considered for the same position didn't mean that we couldn't be friends. If the manager chose me to start at shortstop, which happened most years, the other guy might be my backup. Or I might find him playing next to me at second base, and he'd be my partner in double-play combinations. If I was unkind to him when we were trying out for short, he'd remember that, and we might not be able to perform well together. And of course, in the end, that would be bad for the team. So as a matter of routine, I tried to build a good relationship with the guy who was taking grounders next to me in spring training.

In 1931, Yankee shortstop Lyn Lary was perched on first base when Lou Gehrig came up to the plate with two outs. Lou hit a home run to center field that bounced out of stands and back into the glove of the outfielder. Looking over his shoulder as he rounded second base, Lary only saw the ball go into the fielder's glove, and thinking that was the third out, he trotted past third base and right into the Yankee dugout. Gehrig, meanwhile, was trotting around the bases with his head down and didn't notice what Lary had done. When he reached home plate, the umpires called him out for passing a base runner. So Gehrig's homer was wiped off the books.

After the game, Lou refused to blame his shortstop. "A dozen mistakes are made in every game," he said. "Anybody can pull a boner."

Don't get me wrong, though. I still tried to catch every ground ball and execute every throw to first base flawlessly. I also wanted the coaches who were looking on to say something like "Cal is much better than this new guy. The kid might have some raw talent, but he can't do what Ripken does."

In later years, even though I had established myself as a veteran, I never took it for granted that I had a job. I competed with the guys who were being considered for my position, but I still shared my knowledge and experience with them. When I showed a willingness to teach, they began to ask questions. And when I answered those questions, I found that my willingness to do so was very much appreciated—by the rookies, by the coaches, and by the manager. I always felt secure enough in my job, and confident enough in my ability, to believe that it didn't matter how many of my techniques I shared. After all, the other guy still had to apply what I was sharing in order to be successful. And in the end, if he could do so, it would help the team.

Usually when you display kindness and decency to your teammates, it will be returned. And I always felt that, if a rookie remembered how I worked with him, he might pass it along in later years. Actually, that's what I was doing. I never forgot how, in 1981, veterans like Doug DeCinces, Mark Belanger, and Eddie Murray went out of the way to share their expertise with me. In spring training, for example, Eddie used to hang out at shortstop after he'd taken his own ground balls at first base. That's when he befriended me.

Eddie Murray turned out to be something of a natural older brother. He not only taught me how to relax, he coached me in the basics of being a big leaguer. Just a few of the things he used to say included, keep it simple, stay within yourself, teammates come first, no false hustle, no complaints, and do your best. Every young person needs to hear those things from a more experienced person. Through his actions, Eddie also demonstrated how important it was to be in the lineup every day. If it was late in the game, and we were either leading or trailing by a huge margin, he did not want to come out. "I want to play the eighth inning!" he'd tell the manager. "I want to play the ninth inning, too. Don't take me out. This is my job!"

Team chemistry is forged in many different ways. I firmly believe that the best way to build rapport and connections is by relating directly to people. And it came naturally for me to do so in a playful manner, whether it was through high jinks in the locker room, shenanigans with my teammates, or exchanging playful punches with clubhouse attendants. My way also had the side benefit of creating a tension-free, loose environment.

In the minor leagues, for instance, I was always pulling

pranks on my buddy John "T-Bone" Shelby. I would put Vaseline in his shower shoes, for instance. And when he'd get a new pair, I'd nail them to the floor, or to the ceiling. Of course, he'd always get me back one way or another. These little pranks were harmless fun, and I always felt they built camaraderie among the guys. We were always waiting to see what happened next.

When I made it to the majors, I roomed with catcher Rick Dempsey, who was a real practical joker. On road trips, the two of us used to go after the radio play-by-play announcer, Tom Marr. On one road trip, we'd just finished playing the Indians and were checking into the hotel in the next city when Tom passed me in the hall and said, "Hey, how's zero-for-Cleveland Cal doing?" Well, Rick and I decided to get him back for that. So we gained access to his hotel room and started setting up a bunch of booby traps. We put pine needles under his mattress, soaked his pillows in water, and were in the process of setting up small trash can filled with water above the door when we heard Tom put his key in the latch. He had forgotten his coat and was coming back for it. I dived into the closet and closed the door, while Dempsey jumped into the shower stall.

Tom could tell that we had been in the room setting some traps, but he didn't realize we were still in there. When he opened the closet door to get his jacket, I yelled, "Boo!" He jumped three feet in the air, I pushed him onto the bed and bolted out the door. Then he chased me down the hall, yelling, "I'm going to get you guys! I'm going to get you!"

While I was making my escape down the back stairwell, Rick

repositioned himself from the shower to the closet. So when Tom got back to his room, he opened the closet door one more time to get his jacket. This time, it was Rick who yelled "Boo!" and pushed Tom down on the bed and ran out of the room. I swear, only Dempsey could have thought of that.

After the New York Yankees won the 1928 World Series, Lou Gehrig was part of a group of players who made their way into the rooms of owner Jacob Ruppert, businessman Fred Wattenberg, and field manager Miller Huggins. Babe Ruth stole Ruppert's pajama top, Gehrig took a pair of Wattenberg's pants, and one of the other guys took Huggins's false teeth.

We liked Tom Marr a lot. He was a friend of ours, and all of our high jinks were designed, in part, to make him feel part of the team. And I believe he did. Practical jokes can, if done right, serve a good purpose for the continuity of the team. But sometimes, they can be counterproductive. Let me give you a quick example.

In the major leagues, there was something called a rookie prank that, when I first came up, was not practiced in the Orioles organization. But slowly, as other players came in from other teams, it was brought in to our clubhouse. The prank went something like this: On the last game of a road trip, players had forty-five minutes to do interviews, get showered, dressed, and on the bus for the trip to the airport. Personal luggage had already been carried out of the hotel, so each of the players would wear his travel clothes to that day's game.

Well, the first-year guys would often open their locker to find that their clothes had been replaced with something, shall we say, in a style to which they were not accustomed. It might be flared seventies bell-bottom pants, a polka-dot tie, a plaid shirt, a polyester jacket that was too small, and a pair of platform shoes. With only a couple of minutes left to make the bus, and virtually no one left in the locker room, the new guy would have no choice but to wear this outfit on the plane.

I didn't advocate these initiations for first-year players. But I must admit the first time I saw one was kind of amusing, because it was done in a good-natured, respectful manner. With time, however, these pranks escalated to a point where they were no longer funny, at least not to me.

I remember one year when big, strong Armando Benitez opened up his locker to find a wig, high-heel shoes, and a dress. Well, he had no intention of dressing up in drag, so he pitched a fit and refused to get on the team bus. Actually, I advised Armando not to give in and even offered to pay his plane fare to the next city. Finally, the manager forced the culprits to give Armando back his clothes.

Sometimes people pull practical jokes that are demeaning and degrading. When that happens, it becomes counterproductive to the individual and to the team as a whole. There was no need to embarrass or humiliate one of our teammates, I felt. The main object was to make guys feel like they were part of the team, not alienate them from the group.

Good-natured fun is important in building relationships and strong bonds. After all, baseball is a team sport. No single player could ensure success for an entire season. We needed each other. When one guy was on a hot streak, rather than being jealous, the rest of us had to cheer him on. When another was in a slump, we needed to encourage and support him. It was him today. But it might be us tomorrow. When one succeeds, we all succeed.

I always valued open communication in the clubhouse. When we had good games, we talked about *why* they were good games. When we were in the middle of a losing streak, we tried to figure out what our problems were, cope with them, and regroup. By speaking to each other regularly, we cut misunderstandings to a minimum, and that promoted stability on the team. If people don't mistrust each other, they're more likely to perform well together.

Good communication and good teamwork don't just happen. You have to work at it. Every team needs a couple of leaders in the clubhouse. When I was young, Eddie Murray was one of those guys. In later years, as a veteran, I tried to provide the leadership by keeping the clubhouse upbeat, and by setting a good example—just as Eddie used to do.

My teammate and good friend B. J. Surhoff told me after I retired that the players had much more respect for me than they ever let on. "If we were banged up, tired, or otherwise just not going well," he said, "the manager would come up and ask us if we wanted a day off. It was easy to say yes, to beg out of the lineup. But you set the example for all of us. Because you wanted to be in the lineup every day, so did I. As a matter of fact, you inspired me to play all 162 games in a season. I'd never done that before. The truth is, we all felt that way. I became a better ballplayer because of it. And we became a better team."

> "Lou was the perfect team man. He set an example for the rest of us. If this towering star was willing to obey his manager and approach the sport with the same deadly seriousness that Joe McCarthy did, then who were we to do any less?"
> —TOMMY HENRICH
> **Yankee outfielder and teammate of Lou Gehrig**

B.J.'s comment really meant a lot to me. I don't think you can be successful in anything without the help, friendship, and goodwill of other people. Your teammates and colleagues rely on you, and you rely on them. More than anything else in the world, I wanted to be counted on by my teammates to be in the lineup every day.

THE COMPETITION

The guy on first gets the steal sign, he's running on the pitch, and I'm moving over to second to take the throw from the catcher. But the batter fouls the ball off. "Hey, foul ball," I'll say to the runner. "Stand up. Stand up. You're okay."

Nine times out of ten, before the runner heads back to

first, he'll say something like "Hey, thanks, man. I appreciate that."

Some infielders won't give the guy a warning. They'll let the runner slide into the base and figure out what happened on his own. But if you give that guy a heads-up, you've built a small bit of trust that might be of use later in the game. Suppose, for instance, that this same runner gets on first again. Only this time he steals as part of the front end of a hit-and-run play. The batter is thrown out at first, but the runner makes it to second base. If there's some question in my mind whether that was really a hit-and-run, I'll say something to the runner: "Hey, you really got a bad jump for a straight steal."

"Oh, no, Cal," he'll respond, "that was a hit-and-run all the way." So I take that information and put it in my memory bank. I'll remember the hitter at the plate, the runner on first, and the number of outs. And the next time that situation comes up, I'll be looking for the hit-and-run.

There's a wealth of information you can glean from members of the competition. In order to gain access to it, however, you have to build relationships. Warning a guy to stand up on a foul ball is a little thing that can help in the long run. But you have to be consistent. If you mislead a base runner during a key moment in the game, you'll lose all credibility. Word will get around and they'll never trust you again—and that's not just on their team, it's the entire league.

Every kid whoever played Little League baseball has tried the hidden-ball trick. You know how it works. The infielder pretends he's thrown the ball back to the pitcher when, in fact, he still has it snug in his glove. And when the runner leads off the base, he gets tagged out. It doesn't happen very often in major league baseball, mostly because the runners are too smart.

Yankee shortstop Frank Crosetti often pulled off the hidden-ball trick when there was a runner on second base. In order to distract the runner, Lou Gehrig would yell encouragement to the pitcher, who was staring at the batter and pretending the ball was in his glove. When the runner took his lead, Crosetti would tag him out. If it was the third out of an inning, Lou would laugh and then run over and hug Crosetti. Lou Gehrig loved the hidden-ball trick.

I can't stand the hidden-ball trick. That runner on base trusts you to a point. But when you get him out like that, you embarrass him in front of everybody else. Then he'll never trust you again about anything. And just like misleading a base runner during a key moment in the game, you can only do it once.

I believe there are more honorable ways to gain an advantage. If you're the hitter, and the pitcher tips his hand with a face gesture or a hand movement, or if you're playing the in-field and you decipher a bunt sign from the third-base coach—you're gathering data by guessing. That's not cheating or embarrassing anybody. It's part of the game.

In the mid-1980s, everything started coming together for me on the baseball field. I was fielding well, and at the plate I was hotter than a firecracker. During the third or fourth game of a series in Anaheim, Ruppert Jones hit a double, and while he was standing on second base, he smiled and said, "Cal, you haven't taken a bad swing since you've been here. You really look comfortable with your hands away from your body like that."

I knew Ruppert fairly well, and I don't think he was trying to throw me off. Rather, he was just making an astute observation and complimenting me in the process. But the next time up to bat, I started to overanalyze the position of my hands, and sure enough, my bat cooled off. As a matter of fact, for a while, I couldn't hit anything. Being affected by Ruppert's remark was my own fault. But if I thought he had done it intentionally, I would have been angry. It violated my own personal code of honor.

Over the years, I've been sensitive to the fact that people think differently and have varying codes by which they live. And that's good. We should respect everybody's point of view. But that doesn't mean we can't get into a discussion with someone when we disagree with them.

Shortly after retiring from baseball, I found myself in the company of businessman and financier Donald Trump at Mar-A-Lago in Palm Beach, Florida. He looked at me playfully and said, "Hey, Cal, I'd love to take your money on the golf course sometime."

"You must be pretty good at golf," I replied.

"I'm okay, but I beat a lot of guys who are better than I am, because they aren't strong enough mentally."

"You mean you play mind games with them?"

"That's part of golf, isn't it?" said Trump.

"Well, I don't think so. If I'm going to measure my golfing ability against yours, I want you to have your best game. Then if I beat you, I know I'm a better golfer. But if I'm playing mind games and I beat you, all it proves is that I'm better at playing mind games."

"C'mon, Cal, that's all part of the sport. It's how you handle the pressure."

"I don't think so. That would be like me waiting for Derek Jeter to come to second base and then saying, 'Derek, you're swinging the bat very well. I've never seen you be on every pitch like you are right now. Keep going, you really look comfortable with your hands up there away from your body.' So then, Derek would be thinking about his hands. I will have planted a thought that might mess him up. Not only that, but I'd never get any information out of Derek again, because he'd never trust me again."

I don't know if I convinced Donald Trump of anything, but I think I made my point. And I certainly respected his view on what we were discussing, because a lot of people feel exactly the way he does. However, I always felt strongly about honor and a code of competition. Whomever I found myself up against, whether it was in baseball or golf, I wanted that guy to play his best game. If I won the game, I'd feel good. If I didn't—well, I'd get him the next time. I'm certain that code went all the way back to playing canasta when I was a kid. Don't cheat your blind grandma.

I've taken that same general approach into business. Time after time in baseball, I noticed that many general managers gloated when they made a trade that was good for their team, but bad for the other team. Well, that is a win-lose situation that might be good in the short term, but it will come back to haunt you in the long term. You can only do that once, maybe twice, before word starts to spread around the league. The other teams will be hesitant to deal with you because they aren't sure you're not going to try to screw them.

On the other hand, if you make a deal where both you and the other team get exactly what you both need, you're setting a precedent that will help you in the long term. Word will spread that you're an honorable person to deal with, your reputation will be enhanced, and prospective partners will seek you out. By creating a win-win situation, you ensure both short-term *and* long-term success.

MANAGEMENT

During my major league career, I had nine different field managers, a dozen different general managers, and four different ownership groups. And it was the same every time a new person stepped through the door. They brought in new people to help him run the show, and all of a sudden I was wondering if they thought I had value, if I'd continue at my position, or if I'd even have a job at the end of the day.

Lou Gehrig had only two managers in his major league career. Although Miller Huggins and Joe McCarthy were about as different as two people could be, Lou got along extraordinarily well with both of them.

Huggins was patient, pleasant, and insightful. He spent a great deal of time teaching, advising, and supporting Lou in the early years of his career.

Joe McCarthy was a tough taskmaster with an intense desire to win. He was known for hammering into players his "Ten Commandments of Baseball," which included: Do not alibi on bad hops; Always run them out; Do not quit; and Do not fight too much with the umpires.

Just about everybody I know has had to deal with the same thing in the companies they work for. And they've had those same feelings and concerns. Actually, my friends have often asked me how I survived so many changes. "Cal, how did you become the constant when everything else changed around you?" they'd ask. "On-field managers, alone, you averaged a new one every two years. How did you do it?"

My response was usually the same: "I helped the manager manage me."

I didn't mean that in a glib or condescending way. Rather, I just didn't want to be a guy who sat back and had to wonder all the time about what my future was going to be. So I decided to take a proactive approach. On the first day of spring training, I'd walk up to the new manager and congratulate him. Then I'd sit down in his office and ask a simple starter question, something like "How do you see my spring training going?"

Most managers would respond by saying, "Well, Cal,

you've been doing this for some time, now. How do you see it unfolding?"

Ninety-nine percent of players can't go in and start that conversation. They view it as confrontational. Later in my career, some of my younger teammates would come up and ask me all kinds of questions they should have been asking the manager. "Why won't he play me?" "Why won't he bring me in to pitch?" "Why did he pinch-hit for me?" Most of the time, the guys were trying to get some reassurance and understanding as to their own situation. I would usually advise them to go directly to the manager. "You don't have to go in there and yell," I'd say. "Just ask for some time, tell him something's bothering you, and start a conversation."

I was amazed how many people searched for answers to simple questions without going directly to the manager, who was the source of most information. To me, it was just proper communication. And it almost always worked. Once I took the initiative to get a dialogue going, I could understand what the expectations were of me, what the new manager felt about my consecutive-games streak, and whether he saw me as having value to the team as an everyday player. Just knowing those things, whether the answers were good or bad, took away a lot of the doubt in my mind and allowed me to focus on my job.

I don't mean to suggest that it's a snap to get what you want out of a manager. That's not true at all. Every skipper I had to deal with was different. At first, Earl Weaver was intimidating to me. Of course, I was just a kid and he was my dad's age. But if you wanted to know something, you really had to ask him. He was the one in charge and everybody knew it. However, because Earl talked to me as much as he did, I could be honest and candid with him. And I know he not only respected that, but also wanted it from all his players.

My second manager was Joe Altobelli, who took over in 1983 after Earl retired. Joe had spent eleven years as a coach and manager in the Baltimore farm system. In the big leagues, he had been a coach with the New York Yankees and a manager for three years with the San Francisco Giants. We got along great. I treated him with respect and that's the way he treated me. Actually, I was very impressed with Joe's ability to recognize what worked well, leave it alone, and then fix only what needed fixing. That year, we won ninety-eight games during the regular season and went on to win the World Series. That's a credit not only to Earl Weaver, who originally forged the team, but to Joe Altobelli for keeping it going and improving on it.

My seventh manager was Baltimore Orioles veteran Davey Johnson, who took over in 1996, the year after I broke Lou Gehrig's record. Davey was a top-notch manager. He won everywhere he went. But we had a few issues when he was my manager. During his first season, B. J. Surhoff, who was playing third, got hurt. Right away, Davey said he was considering placing B.J. on the disabled list, moving me to third base, and putting Manny Alexander at shortstop. Well, that really caught me off guard, so I came in early the next day to talk to him about it. We went out to the batting cages at Camden

Yards to be alone. "Davey," I said, "you know I haven't played third in nearly fifteen years."

"Yes, I'm aware of that," he replied. "But I'm sure you can handle it."

"If you put Manny at short, then there will be two guys in positions that they haven't played in a long time."

"Yes, I know."

"What are you going to do when B.J. comes back?" I asked.

"Well, I'm not sure, yet."

We had a long and pleasant talk, after which I asked, "Do you feel urgent about making this move?"

"No, it was just an idea," he replied.

"Then can I make a suggestion?"

"Sure."

"I'd really appreciate it if we didn't make this move while we're playing at home. Could we think about it some more and meet again tomorrow to continue the discussion?"

"Okay, good idea," said Davey. "But I can't guarantee there won't be any leaks."

"Why not?"

"Because it's been discussed in meetings."

"Okay, how about this. If somebody comes and asks you about it, you can say we've discussed it, but right now it's just a thought."

"Yeah, that's a good idea."

So after we ended our conversation, I went into the cages and took some batting practice. But Davey walked into the middle of a group of reporters and said something to the effect of "I know you guys are going to find out about this anyway, so I'll tell you now. I'm considering moving Cal to third. We've talked about it and he's amenable. Cal's a good team player."

Right after that, all the reporters came over to me and started asking about the move to third. Caught off guard, and not wanting to make any mistakes, I just said I didn't have any comment at this time. Well, of course, they didn't like that, and the next day a bunch of negative articles about me appeared in the media.

Afterward, I walked into Davey's office and blasted him: "Look, I don't know what you're doing, but I've been around long enough to know that it's some sort of game."

"No, you don't understand—"

"No, I understand. You said *this* and you did *that!*" And then I stormed out of his office.

Davey and I eventually patched things up. As a matter of fact, several days later, just before our next road game, he told me that he had decided to stay with me at shortstop. I guess I experienced a sense of relief, because I hit three home runs in the game that night.

Working with managers was certainly a challenge. But dealing with owners and executives was another matter altogether—especially when it came to working out contracts. After the 1991 season, which may have been my best overall year, I was close to signing a five-year contract in spring training. Eli Jacobs was the owner of the Orioles at that time, and Larry Lucchino was the president. Negotiations fell off at the end of 1992 spring training and ended up dragging on through the entire regular season. As the discussions went up and down, so did my emotions, as well my performance on the field. When the negotiations looked good, I relaxed and played better. When things got bad, I became tense and didn't play well.

The entire 1992 season was a terrible roller coaster for me. But I eventually learned to anticipate such things and get my contract negotiations out of the way before the season started. Of course, whenever I was negotiating a contract, the issue of loyalty always came up. Many people believe that players should have a blind loyalty to the team they play for. But I believe loyalty is a two-way street. It's also a commitment issue. It was easy for me to commit to playing in Baltimore. I grew up there, I lived there, and I wanted to raise my children there. So I did the best I could with contract negotiations. In doing so, I may have taken a little less money, but at least I had the money issues behind me. After all, I was there mainly to play baseball.

In 1927, Lou Gehrig's salary was $6,000 per year, compared to Babe Ruth's $70,000. The most Lou ever made in a year was $39,000 in 1938. That year, Joe DiMaggio, in only his second season with the Yankees, was paid $25,000.

Lou did not look at baseball as a business. It was much more than that to him. He disliked contract negotiations and never threatened to walk out if he wasn't paid more money. If he had held tough against the Yankee owner, he could probably have received a much higher salary. But it just wasn't in his nature.

At the end of the day, I realized that money wasn't everything to me. Living where I wanted to live, being part of a great organization, and maintaining the long-term business and personal friendships in my hometown were the most important elements to my personal happiness, and to that of my family.

I'm sure I could have made more money had I jumped full force into the free agent market. But to tell you the truth, it just wouldn't have been worth it to me.

THERE WAS ONLY ONE TIME in my career when I seriously considered leaving the Baltimore Orioles. That was in the first few months of the 1988 season. As usual, I was in the starting lineup on Opening Day, my brother Billy was playing second base, and my dad was in his second year as manager. But after losing the first six games, Dad was called into the owner's office for what he believed would be a discussion about player moves. Instead, he was fired.

I felt bad—bad for my father, bad for my brother, bad for me, and bad for the Orioles. After all, Dad had been with the organization for thirty-one years. Stunned by the news, he said he was going to take a couple of weeks off to decide whether to accept another job with the club.

Immediately after I heard what had happened, I wanted to blame somebody. Most of my teammates and friends called it a "raw deal," and somebody even told me that Dad's firing was the earliest in a season for a manager in major league history. It seemed that upper management just didn't want to undertake the hard work of rebuilding our baseball team. Rather, they had decided to try for a quick fix. Of course, it didn't work. Nineteen eighty-eight was the year we set the record for most losses at the start of a season (twenty-one, which means that we lost fifteen more after they fired Dad)— and we ended up losing 107 overall.

I tried to keep my emotions under control, and as far as the media was concerned, I basically just shut up. "As a player, I have no opinion," I commented. "As a son, I'll keep my opinions to myself." In a subsequent interview, I did go so far as to say that my father had been wronged. But that was about it.

It didn't take long for trade rumors to start swirling. I heard there was supposed to be a blockbuster deal with Boston in the works—four or five of the Red Sox young prospects for me. The front office assumed I wanted out, and if they were going to lose me, they wanted to get something in return. If I'd had to make the decision right after Dad was fired, I would probably have been all for the trade. But several factors persuaded me to go to the Orioles ownership and tell them I wanted to stay in Baltimore.

First of all, I had just gotten married, and I wanted to stay at home and raise a family. Second, the man who took over for my father as manager was a good guy with whom I already had an established relationship. Frank Robinson softened my initial negative reactions by calling Billy and me into his office on the day that Dad was fired. (At that time, Frank had been serving in upper management with the club.) The first thing he said was that he had not lobbied for the job. Rather, he had received a phone call from Edward Bennett Williams, who had asked him to take over the club. "I was stunned by the question," said Frank, "and I told him that your father was a good manager and he deserved to be given more than just a year and six games to prove himself." Frank went on to say that Mr. Williams said he had made up his mind, and if Frank didn't take the job, he'd find someone else. "Well, I didn't want that, so I took the job," Frank said.

I could have harbored resentment against Frank Robinson—and believe me, I wanted to. But I was impressed with the way he talked to Billy and me. I also wanted to take the high road and find a way to play the hand I was dealt. In essence, I gave Frank the benefit of the doubt, and he did not let me down. Not only did he later help me out of a terrible batting slump, but he also brought back my father as his third-base coach. In addition, whenever the question came up about my consecutive-games streak, Frank Robinson never hesitated. "The easiest part of my job is knowing who I'm going to pencil in at shortstop every day," he told the press. "I wish I had a whole team of Cal Ripkens."

ON JUNE 25, 1988, I played in my 1,000th consecutive game. Less than two years later, I would pass Joe Sewell, Billy Williams, and Steve Garvey on the record list. Then only two guys would be ahead of me: Everett Scott and Lou Gehrig.

EIGHT RIPKEN PRINCIPLES

6. TRUSTING RELATIONSHIPS

1. It doesn't matter how many of your techniques you share with the other guy. He still has to apply them.
2. When you display kindness and decency to your teammates, it will be returned.
3. Good-natured fun is important in building relationships and strong bonds.
4. If you speak to your teammates regularly, misunderstandings will be cut to a minimum, and that promotes stability on the team.
5. There's a wealth of information you can you can glean from members of the competition. In order to gain access to it, however, you have to build relationships.
6. Don't sit back and wonder what your future is going to be. Open a dialogue. Help the manager manage you.
7. Money isn't everything. Living where you want to live, being part of a great organization, and maintaining long-term friendships are the most important elements of personal happiness.
8. Find a way to take the high road and play the hand you're dealt.

On May 19, 1998, in Yankee Stadium, an ugly and lengthy brawl took place that some veterans present remember as one of the nastiest they ever witnessed. And I was right in the middle of the whole thing.

Going into this game, the Orioles had lost six straight. But we took an early lead and there was a general air of optimism that we were finally going to break our losing streak. In the bottom of the eighth inning, however, Bernie Williams hit an upper-deck, three-run homer off our ace reliever, Armando Benitez, to put the Yanks ahead 7–5. Armando was understandably upset that he had given up the lead, especially in such dramatic fashion. But no one expected what happened next.

When Yankee first baseman Tino Martinez stepped into the batter's box, Armando was still fuming on the mound. Losing his cool, Ar-

mando proceeded to drill Tino in the upper back with one of his 102 mph fastballs. The home plate umpire, Drew Coble, immediately waved his arm and threw Benitez out of the game. Tino wanted to charge the mound, but he was in such pain that all he could manage was a couple of steps before he doubled over. When Yankee players, led by six-foot-six-inch Darryl Strawberry, began pouring out of the dugout, Armando defiantly turned toward them, dropped his glove, and beckoned them onward.

Without even realizing it, I suddenly found myself positioned (along with our first baseman and catcher) on the first line of defense between Armando and the Yankees. I didn't like what my pitcher had done, but he was still my teammate and I wasn't going to let the Yankees have him. There was some initial pushing and shoving, but things really escalated when players from both bullpens charged in from the outfield. Yankee pitchers Graeme Lloyd and Jeff Nelson reached Armando from behind and punches began to fly. As the whole group rolled toward our dugout along the third-base line, Darryl Strawberry saw an opening and threw a haymaker at Armando. When Strawberry's momentum carried him down into the dugout, Alan Mills (one of our relief pitchers) slugged him back. The next thing I knew, I was in the dugout pinning Darryl against the bench in an effort to keep him from retaliating. Even though I was holding on to him with all my might, he kept flailing at both Mills and Benitez. The whole incident was an ugly scene, and one in which I'm not proud to have taken a part.

After about ten minutes, things calmed down. Benitez went into the clubhouse, Yankee manager Joe Torre led Strawberry back to the Yankees' dugout, and the game eventually resumed. (The Yanks won that game, by the way.) In the postgame interviews, a lot of heat was directed at Armando. I felt that he had made a mistake in the heat of competi-

tion, but others on the team, including management, came down on him pretty hard.

Once all the reporters left the locker room, I looked over at Armando and saw him sitting hunched over with his head in his locker. Nobody was talking to him, and clearly he was in pain. After everybody had left the clubhouse, I went over, sat down next to Armando, and draped my arm around his shoulder. "Hey, it's okay," I said. "It's okay. That wasn't the first brawl in baseball and it certainly won't be the last. People lose their tempers in the heat of competition. I've done it before. Everybody has."

Then I tried to make Armando laugh a little bit. "I've got to give you credit, buddy," I said. "To drill Martinez with your fastball right here in Yankee Stadium surrounded by all those hostile fans—man, that took big cojones!" Armando did smile slightly, more so than anything, I believe, because he knew I was trying to cheer him up.

"Listen, Armando, we all make mistakes," I said. "You made a mistake out there today. It's not the end of the world. Everything is going to be all right. Just put it behind you. Don't worry about it."

In the off-season, Armando was traded to the New York Mets. When I saw him in spring training down in Florida, he came up to me to say good-bye and thank me for my friendship. As we shook hands, he slipped me a small gift, which I opened later. It was a gold ring with the number 8 in the center. No one had ever done anything like that for me before. Armando's expression of gratitude and thanks was really heartfelt. And I will never forget it.

CHAPTER 7

LIFE MANAGEMENT

*Personal happiness is most related to the people in your life, what you
do for a living, and how you feel about yourself. For me, baseball
and community involvement brought those three things together. If I
was happy in one, I was happy in the others.*

E arly in my career, I was told that a professional baseball
player's legs were the first things to go. So I made up my
mind to stay in shape during the off-season. At first, I worked
in the gym, lifted weights, and jogged. All those things were
okay, but they lacked the fun and competitiveness I enjoyed.
To try something different, I signed up for racquetball lessons, where the better a player is, the less the workout, because he can more precisely place the ball. "I'm not interested
in seeing you kill the shot," I told my instructor. "I want you
to work me out. Hit the ball so that the points are long and I
get run around the court." In essence, I paid the guy to beat
the crap out of me.

I received a good workout from racquetball, but it still didn't provide the fun and competitiveness I was looking for. I needed to get other people involved, so I started thinking of team sports as an alternative. Basketball seemed the most natural fit for me, because I'd been playing it since I was a kid. During winter, I used to shoot hoops on our driveway for hours—until my hands were frozen. "Don't let me hear you complain," my mom used to say. "When you grow up and become a major league baseball player, you can buy a farm and convert the barn into a gym."

In due course, I joined the Orioles off-season basketball team, which was manned by players who lived in the area, including Mike Boddicker, Tim Stoddard, Al Bumbry, Rich Dauer, and several others. We practiced in the gym at Bryn Mawr School and traveled around playing in various charity tournaments. Unfortunately, basketball can be a very physical game, and the injuries started to mount up. One of our starting pitchers, for instance, tore his Achilles tendon in a pickup game. I suffered a dislocated finger after being slammed into a wall. Finally, Orioles president Larry Lucchino ordered an end to the Orioles team on the grounds that the games were just too rough. Of course, he had a point. But I still wanted to play basketball. So I set up my own pickup games.

At first, we continued to play at Bryn Mawr—at least one to three nights a week. But soon I did exactly what my mom had told me I could do back when I was a kid. I put a big addition on my house, a gymnasium that included batting cages, a weight room, a locker room, and, of course, a full-size basketball court. It was a splurge, but I felt if it extended my career by just one year, it would have paid for itself. And during my next contract negotiation, I insisted on a clause allowing me to play basketball in the off-season.

> **When once asked what he was going to do in the off-season, Lou Gehrig responded, "I plan to play a lot of basketball."**

PHYSICAL FITNESS

It's pretty obvious that athletes need to be in good physical condition to do their jobs. While baseball is not as physically grueling as basketball, football, or hockey, each season, I still had to play 162 games in 175 days, which is certainly a test of any athlete's stamina. In order to be able to play every game, I felt I had to take good care of myself not just during the season, but year-round. That came easily for me, because I was raised with a father who was a professional athlete, and a mother who knew how to take care of him.

Before I left home for the minor leagues, both my parents advised me to eat well. "Don't be afraid to spend your money on food," said Dad. "It is fuel for your body. You will not be able to play every day or do what is necessary if you don't eat right." And my mom armed me with a folder full of recipes (hamburger casserole, eye of round roast, turkey pot pies, etc.) and cooking advice about the basic food groups. "Learn how to cook for yourself," she recommended.

Through the minor leagues and up into the big leagues, I did, in fact, learn how to cook nutritious meals that included fruits, vegetables, meat, potatoes, fish, and poultry. I also made it a point never to miss breakfast, and to eat a full meal five to six hours before night games. Eating two meals before each ball game was a consistent routine throughout my career.

As far as physical conditioning, Dad set me straight right from the beginning, saying, "Baseball will wear and tear on you, so be in the best shape of your life on the first day of spring training. I guarantee you that, no matter what you do, it'll be all downhill from there." I certainly took that advice to heart, and by running, lifting weights, and playing racquetball and basketball, I almost always reported to Florida in top physical condition. It seemed pretty simple to me: Take care of yourself and you will not only play your best, you'll also reduce the chances of injury. That thought became my guide for twenty-one major league baseball seasons.

"I was never very far out of shape."

—**LOU GEHRIG**

As I got older, I had to adjust my off-season exercise and maintenance programs in order to handle the inevitable aging process. In general, I listened to my body as I carefully devised workout regimens for every day of the week. I hit more baseballs off my tee and in the batting cage. I threw more baseballs against the wall. I lifted heavier weights. But I also made certain that I never taxed my body so far that it caused me problems. My goals were to stay at my optimum weight, keep my maximum strength, and make sure my muscles were properly toned.

Even though I always showed up in great shape for spring training, the first few weeks of running, stopping, and turning in cleats on a sandy field usually left me with aches and pains in my legs. Except for that, Dad was absolutely right— the physical conditioning was all downhill. And that, in turn, allowed me to really focus on my batting skills and infield training. By the time the regular season got rolling, I was always ready to go. At that point, I would shorten my maintenance program, because the primary focus shifted to games. If I needed to rest, I listened to my body and rested. I also monitored my weight, which tended to go up slightly as the season wore on.

Most people would, I believe, admit there is a direct connection between physical fitness and mental strength. While I was playing baseball, however, I don't think I ever appreciated how profound that relationship really was. But within a year of retiring, I clearly noticed a difference. One day, I was wearing a baseball uniform. The next day I was in a suit. And wanting to move quickly into the business world, I changed my entire routine. In particular, I did not want to be tied to the gym anymore, so I stopped working out so often. As a result, I gained about fifteen pounds that first year. Worse, however, was the fact that I didn't have the same stamina or mental energy I used to have. That's when it became clear to me just how important physical conditioning was in my ability to show up for work and perform well every single day. So I went back on a more regular exercise program, and sure enough, the energy level to which I had become accustomed returned. And it made all the difference in the world as to how I approached my new career in business.

I wish I had the exact answer or formula for achieving success on a daily basis, but I really don't. There were days when, physically, I was 100 percent, but because I was not mentally prepared, I experienced some of the worst days of my career. And then there were days when I was only 60 percent physically and had some of the best days of my career. It was on days like that, when I really felt my back was up against the wall, that I told myself it was time to step forward and ratchet up my concentration and focus. Many people don't do that. When things get tough, and they get broken down physically, they have a tendency to run away. The great football coach Vince Lombardi said it best: "Fatigue makes cowards of us all."

In order to succeed every day, you need to be physically fit. Physical toughness, in turn, leads to mental toughness. And when you combine both, you not only reduce the chances of injury and sickness, you increase your stamina and your ability to persevere through virtually any storm that comes along.

After my retirement, many people mentioned to me that they believed the secret to being at work every day was more of a mental achievement than a physical one. Well, they were exactly right. The secret of everything you do is in between your ears.

ACHIEVING BALANCE

About five years into my career as a major league baseball player, Eddie Murray and I got off the team plane on a Sunday night and headed over to the bus that would take us out to satellite parking. We'd done this dozens of times before after returning from road trips. Both us were single and we kind of stuck together. But this one night, when I saw all of my teammates' families waiting for them, hugging them, and driving them home, I felt that there might be more to life than baseball, after all. When I first began my pro career, I believed it was too difficult to have a family and be on the road so much of the time. After all, I lived that life growing up. My dad was away from home a great deal, and I missed him. So I was pretty adamant that I would not get married until I retired. At least that was the plan.

Fortunately, not long after that Sunday-night plane trip, I met the woman who would change my life for the better. Kelly Geer and I were introduced by her mother and, to make a long story short, the lightning bolt hit me. Happily, Kelly felt the same way about me. We were married on Friday, the thirteenth of November 1987, and took a brief honeymoon in Europe. Kelly wanted to go to Rome and Paris, and while I was happy to oblige, I also wanted to get back home to resume my pickup basketball games and off-season conditioning regime. Luckily, my new wife understood and appreciated my dedication to baseball. Actually, that's one of the reasons I married her.

In September 1933, Lou Gehrig married Eleanor Twitchell. Shortly after the ceremony, a group of motorcycle policemen provided an escort to Yankee Stadium, where Lou played in a game against the Washington Senators. He went 0-4 at the plate, but recorded eight putouts at first base.

I've always believed that the professional and personal aspects of your life are not two different things. If you try to separate them, then you have to ask yourself which is more important. In the grand scheme of things, it's all important. Your life is your life. Of course, it's not always easy to achieve a balance. You have to set priorities, and sometimes concessions and sacrifices have to be made. But with a little bit of planning, and an understanding spouse, it can be done.

When we first got married, it was normal for Kelly to travel with me on road trips. She enjoyed going to other cities and seeing the country. Many times, we stayed in a separate hotel from the team. Some clubs believed that bringing your wife on a road trip was taboo. "This is a business trip" was their rule. "No family members." But it was never an issue with the Baltimore Orioles.

The organization you work for has a lot to do with your ability to achieve a balance between the personal and professional sides of your life. Many people work for companies they hate. As a result, it's pretty obvious they aren't going to be happy in their jobs. On the other hand, people who enjoy their workplace tend to be much happier and far more productive. In my case, I'm certain that an appreciation for my employer had a lot to do with my ability to play in so many consecutive games. The Baltimore Orioles was a classy organization. The executives treated us with respect and dignity, and when it came to personal matters, they allowed us to make our own decisions.

As the organization changed, however, I did experience some bumps in the road. To this day, I firmly believe that trust and respect have to be reserved for *people* in the organization, rather than the organization itself. After all, organizations are really only groups of individuals. So when we had a change in ownership, or management, the executives themselves would set the new tone. Sometimes, there were attempts to alter policies I valued. When that happened, I didn't just roll over and take it. One such policy allowed players to drive to games in spring training, rather than take the team bus. I'd been driving myself for years so I'd have the freedom to leave the ballpark and go wherever I wanted after the game. But upper management and club lawyers came out with a memo that basically said, "no more." If one of the players got in a traffic accident, the Orioles could be sued.

Well, I didn't want to give up my freedom in this area, so I went straight to the powers that be and opened a dialogue. "Look, this is important to me," I said. "I've always had this privilege. I've always been responsible. I've never missed a game and I've never been late. Tell me *why* I can't drive." (Remember, I was always the "why" kid.)

Eventually, management reconsidered. They realized that, as a baseball player, my schedule was tough enough as it was.

And based on my actions and past experience, they said I had earned the right to drive. It wasn't as if I received special treatment, though. Other players also stood up after I did, and the rule was finally dropped.

The club was also supportive during the birth of our two children, which, as far as I'm concerned, is a *must* for any business organization. The arrival of our daughter, Rachel, on November 22, 1989, created no conflicts with my schedule, because she was born in the off-season. When Kelly went into the hospital, I stayed with her, slept on the floor, and was there to bond with the baby.

Three and a half years later, when our son, Ryan, was born, time management was a bit more of a challenge. The baby was due in July 1993—right in the heart of the regular season. As the due date approached, there was some debate in the media about whether I should attend the birth if it jeopardized my consecutive-games streak. Even my wife expressed some concern. Of course, I immediately tried to reassure her. "Kelly, this is the most important thing that can happen in our lives. I will be there. I'm one hundred percent sure. Don't worry about it."

I must admit, though, that I had some anxious moments. I definitely wanted to be there for the birth of my son. But I also felt a responsibility to play baseball. I kept scratching my head and thinking that there must be a way to do both. How could I make this right? I must have come up with a dozen or more scenarios. At one point, I think the whole thing actually clouded my judgment. That's when I went in and discussed one possibility with Kelly. "Hypothetically speaking," I said, "if I was to miss a game because of the birth of our child, it would be the right thing to do. I think the entire country would applaud, and I would have no problem with it whatsoever. But keep in mind that this date will be forever stamped in the history of baseball as the day the streak ended. And that would also be our son's birthday. Is that fair to him?"

Well, things have a way of working out. Because Ryan was such a big baby, the doctors decided to get him out two and a half weeks early. It just so happened there was an off day on a road trip between Minnesota and Toronto, which Kelly and I chose for the delivery. I flew out of Minneapolis early on the morning of July 26, 1993, and was there to see my son born. I was able to stay the entire day with Kelly and Ryan before flying to Toronto for the next night's game. Make no mistake about it, though—I did not want to leave. I loved baseball, but this particular separation tore me up inside. Fortunately, my wife encouraged me to get on the plane. And that made it easier.

Now with a family that included a wife and *two* children, I found myself more and more torn about how to achieve a balance between working and being at home. At first, Kelly took the kids on road trips with us. But we had to carry along a lot of extra stuff, which became a real hassle. I also had trouble getting enough sleep. We'd all be in the same hotel room, the fire alarm would go off at midnight and wake everybody up, the baby would cry, and we wouldn't be able to get her back to sleep for a couple of hours. So Kelly and I began to scrutinize my playing schedule more closely and look for alternative ways to be together as a family.

Around this period in my life, time management *really* became critical. If I had the opportunity to fly home on an off day and spend it with my family, I would. But that became risky. What would happen if my flight was delayed? Or if, for some reason, I couldn't get into the next city? Was flying from Toronto to Texas via Baltimore too much? Or should I just go straight to Texas and spend the day there? All these questions came into account when planning my schedule. But in the long run, I tried to make it home as often as I possibly could. Fortunately, I had the means to pay the extra costs. (I never asked the Orioles to pick up any extra charges for my family—plane fare, hotel rooms, etc.)

As the children started to grow, I valued my time with them even more. And even if I got home from a road trip at three or four o'clock in the morning and was dead tired, I would still get up and take Rachel to kindergarten or preschool. That was very, very important to me. After all, what is more important than spending time with your family?

ENJOYING THE JOURNEY

I remember idolizing Brooks Robinson and other professional baseball players when I was a kid. They had a powerful influence over me. I admired them, looked up to them, wanted to be like them. I never forgot that feeling. So when I became a professional baseball player, I felt a responsibility to the people in the stands, especially the kids. That's the main reason I gained a reputation for staying after games and signing autographs until the last kid in line was satisfied.

In order to fulfill that sense of responsibility, I tried to direct my actions in good-hearted ways throughout the community. I believe the desire to help others was born from watching my mother participate in so many activities when I was growing up. Even though she was raising four children, with a husband whose job took him away a lot, she still made the time to help out wherever she could. As far as Mom was concerned, the community in which she lived was part of her life. She was instrumental, for instance, in starting the Boys & Girls Club in Aberdeen. The many things she did for people were not done for fanfare, few people know about them, and she would not want me to speak a lot about them. The bottom line was that my mother believed in helping people. And so do I.

When I was first called up to the Orioles, I probably tried to do a little bit too much. It was hard for me to say no to anybody. A lobbyist in the Washington, D.C., area asked me to help with his campaign to eliminate smoking advertisements in stadiums. And I said yes. I was asked to work the phone bank for the Baltimore Symphony Orchestra telethon with celebrities such as Oprah Winfrey (before she was a national celebrity). And I said yes. I was asked to participate in all kinds of fund-raisers. And I almost always agreed to do so.

I would be remiss if I did not point out that many of my teammates also dedicated themselves to community work in the Baltimore area. As a matter of fact, the Orioles organization, as a whole, was simply fantastic in this regard. Eddie Murray, Scott McGregor, Al Bumbry, and Ken Singleton all bought homes and lived in the area during the off-season—even though they were from other parts of the country. And whenever there was a community-related event in which they could participate, they did. I might point out that, over the years, there was always one person who seemed to outdo us all. With all due respect to my teammates, I think they would agree that Elrod Hendricks was one of the finest humanitarians who ever lived in the Baltimore, Maryland, area. In many ways, he truly was "Mr. Oriole." After spending a team-record thirty-seven years with our club, Elrod died suddenly of a heart attack in 2005. He was a wonderful man. No one could have done more.

After I signed my first long-term contract, one of the first things I did was to sit down and determine where best to apply some of my newfound revenue to help Baltimore. "How can I make a difference?" I recall asking myself. After a great deal of research and thinking, I decided to fund an adult literacy program. Reading helps us unlock knowledge and allows us to learn. We all take for granted the ability to read. But many people, for whatever reason, cannot read well. So I funded an adult literacy center in the heart of the city. The Orioles organization quickly stepped in and added their weight to the project. We created a fund-raising program called Reading, Runs, and Ripken. At first, we pledged money for home runs. But after a while, we realized that a better multiplier was to pledge on RBIs (runs batted in). The program helped a lot of people.

I mention my work in the Baltimore community not because I want everybody to know about it, but because it played a significant role in my ability to persevere through 2,632 consecutive games. Being a real part of my hometown, as opposed to being an outsider, pulled the personal and business aspects of my life together in a way that made them virtually indistinguishable. In turn, that led to stability in my life. When I felt good about what I was doing for Baltimore citizens, I felt good when I was on the ball field, and vice versa. When the Orioles were doing well, it just reenergized my community work.

I also found that helping out in the community came back to me in ways that I never expected or really sought. In 1992, for example, I was surprised by being honored in two significant ways. First, I received the Roberto Clemente Award, which is given annually to "a player who demonstrates the values Clemente displayed in his commitment to community and understanding the value of helping others." (Twenty years earlier, Brooks Robinson had received the second Roberto Clemente Award.) That same year, I was presented with the Lou Gehrig Memorial Award. This was actually three years *before* I broke Lou's record, and it had nothing to do with the streak. The award was established by Lou's college fraternity at Columbia University and is presented annually to "the Major League baseball player who both on and off the field best exemplifies the character of Lou Gehrig." To have my name associated with Roberto Clemente and Lou Gehrig because of my work *off* the ball field, really meant a great deal to me. I don't know if I've ever been more humbled and proud.

Overall, I believe personal happiness is most related to the people in your life, what you do for a living, and how you feel about yourself. For me, baseball and community involvement brought those three things together. If I was happy in one, I was happy in the others.

Life is a journey with many ups and downs—and you have to take the bitter with the sweet. I can't say I'm glad I went through that 0-21 season start back in 1988, but I know I wouldn't have learned as much about myself, or as much about my teammates, without it. Actually, I'm very proud of the way we pulled together and came out of that low point in my career. Learning from the valleys in your life's journey only makes you enjoy and appreciate the peaks that much more.

When I look back on my professional baseball career, I don't think so much about the shining moments when I was standing in front of big crowds in dozens of stadiums around the country. Rather, I think about all the times in the locker room with my teammates. I think about all those bus rides when I was in the minor leagues. I think about all the times I had a breakthrough conversation with somebody. I remember a man who had not been able to read, went through our literacy program, and then thanked me because he'd had no idea what he was missing. And I will never forget how Frank Robinson helped me out of that terrible batting slump, or how Rick Sutcliffe snapped me out of a poor frame of mind with some straight talk. I think of all those little things, and I realize that I had a wonderful career in professional baseball. The truth is that, in one way or another, I enjoyed every minute of it.

"Maybe I'm missing something, but I can't help thinking that people who see life through a train window must be missing something, too. I'm not rich in the accepted sense of the word, but what millionaire can buy my serenity? I have yet to meet the man who can look backward over his shoulder as he passes his thirtieth birthday and say, as I do, 'It's all been worthwhile.'"

—LOU GEHRIG

Dad once told me that money might pay your bills and solve some issues, but it doesn't necessarily make you happy. "It's what you choose to do in life, and how you choose to live, that really make you happy," he said. "Your job should be a vehicle for your life, not your entire life."

Dad was right. If you enjoy the journey, you're going to be more involved. And then you'll always be in the game.

MIDWAY THROUGH MY CAREER, I was involved in a contract negotiation that lasted nearly a year. By the time it was all over, I had secured an agreement that would keep me in Baltimore with an option for four years of postcareer employment. In essence, that contract made me an Oriole for life.

During those negotiations, which were tense at times, I fixed on Brooks Robinson. Throughout his career, he had handled himself so well that nothing negative was ever really said about him. He signed autographs for anyone and everyone. He involved himself sincerely with the community. And he spent twenty-three years with the same team. Not a bad role model.

So when it came down to signing on the dotted line, even though I knew I was leaving money on the table by not testing the free agent market, my final thought was simple: "Be like Brooks." Brooks made me realize that, in my heart, I always wanted to be an Oriole. I never wanted to be anything else.

I also began to realize I might eventually come close to Lou Gehrig's record. A few years earlier, I had played in my 1,308th consecutive game, which moved me past Everett Scott into second place on the all-time list. After that game, I was surprised at how big a deal the media made of the event. "It should be a night for celebrating a streak of skill, perseverance, and outright luck exceeded by only one other player in major league baseball history," wrote one reporter. "Instead, Ripken is cruising past Everett Scott and into controversy." I never really did figure out what that "controversy" was supposed to be about. I was just playing baseball. If I ended up passing Gehrig, what was so bad about that?

I recall being extensively interviewed by a variety of media people after passing Everett Scott. It seemed to be a never-ending string of questions like "What now?" "What's the secret?" "How do you do it?" At that time, one answer I gave seemed to sum up my feelings on the subject: "The biggest myth of the whole streak is the fact that I have played 1,308 games in a row. The most you can play in a row is 162 games, or if you're lucky enough to be in the play-offs and World Series, you add a few more. But then I get four months off just like everybody else. So it's really a string of consecutive *years*."

Lou Gehrig broke his teammate Everett Scott's record on August 17, 1932, making him the official record holder for consecutive games played. During a press interview after the game, Lou reached into his wallet and pulled the box score from June 2, 1925, his first game in the streak. In a celebration at home plate, Lou was presented with a silver statuette by Will Harridge, the American League's president.

When another reporter asked me how I felt about possibly reaching the next plateau, Lou Gehrig's mark of 2,130 consecutive games, I responded as honestly as I could: "I fight against that thought every day of the year. Everybody asks me that question all the time. I just want to continue to approach the game the same way I always have. I'm going to take it one game at a time."

EIGHT RIPKEN PRINCIPLES

7. LIFE MANAGEMENT

1. In order to play in every game, you have to take good care of yourself year-round.
2. As you get older, adjust your exercise and maintenance programs to handle the inevitable aging process.
3. There is a direct connection between physical fitness and mental strength.
4. The secret of everything you do is between your ears.
5. If you try to separate the professional and personal aspects of your life, then you have to ask yourself which is more important. In the grand scheme of things, it's all important.
6. The organization you work for has a lot to do with your ability to achieve a balance between the personal and the professional sides of life.
7. Helping out in your community will come back to you in ways that you never expected.
8. It's what you choose to do in life, and how you choose to live, that really make you happy. Your job should be a vehicle for your life, not your entire life.

One of the most serious threats to my consecutive-games streak came during a game against the Seattle Mariners in Baltimore (officially it was game number 1,790). Mike Mussina was pitching for us, Chris Bosio was on the mound for the Mariners. Bosio was an old-school pitcher, not a bad guy, but he had a reputation of drilling you if the need arose. Well, in the seventh or eighth inning, Mark McLemore and Harold Reynolds tried to bunt a couple of times, and Bosio threw behind both of them. He didn't make contact, but he was definitely sending a message that he didn't appreciate their trying to bunt against him.

The first batter up during our half of the inning was Bill Haselman, who had blasted a home run in his previous at bat. Mussina's first pitch hit him square in the back, and there was no hesitation on Haselman's part. He charged the mound and started wrestling with Mussina. As I ran in from shortstop, my initial inclination was to protect my pitcher. But our first baseman, Paul Carey, got there before me and was already trying to pull Haselman away. Then I realized that the rest of the Mariners were charging out of the dugout, so I turned to stop them. Of course, my first mistake was thinking that I could stop three thousand pounds of beef running toward me. My second mistake was in turning too fast. As I did, my foot slipped and I heard a pop in my right knee. Then I was overrun by the horde and ended up on my back at the bottom of the pile.

I played the rest of the game, and afterward the doctor diagnosed a strain. But when I woke up the next morning, I was shocked at how swollen and painful my knee had become. Barely able to put any weight on it, I called my parents to give them a heads-up. "I hurt myself in the brawl yesterday," I explained, "and might not be able to go tonight." Then I called the team trainer and told him that I was doubtful.

My parents lived in Aberdeen, which is a good forty-five-minute drive from my house. Well, almost exactly forty-five minutes after I hung up the phone, they showed up on my front porch, where I was icing my knee. We discussed the injury, but we didn't talk about the streak, even though I knew it was on all our minds.

As the morning wore on, my goal was to try to play that evening. My regimen was to ice the knee for twenty minutes, walk around the driveway with my mom and dad for twenty minutes, and then rest for twenty minutes. We repeated that routine until midafternoon, when it was time to go to the ballpark. "Hey, this is loosening up a little," I said to my folks. "I might be able to play."

When I arrived at Camden Yards, the trainers worked with me some, then I suited up. First, I went into the batting cages to see if I could swing properly, and second, I took infield practice to see if I could plant and throw properly. Even though, my knee hurt like all get-out, I determined that it was worth trying to play. Sure enough, I was tested immediately. The first play at shortstop was a two-hopper in the hole. I remember thinking, "Okay, it's now or never!" I backhanded the ball, planted all my weight on my right leg, and made the long throw to first for the out. I knew then that, even though it would be painful, I'd be all right. My knee continued to give me trouble over the next couple of weeks until the pain gradually disappeared.

On September 19, 1924, after spending the entire season in the minor leagues, Lou Gehrig was called up to the Yankees for a three-game series in Detroit. With two outs in the eighth inning, the bases loaded, and the Yanks trailing 4–1, Miller Huggins sent Gehrig in as a pinch hitter for Yankee shortstop Everett Scott. Lou rapped a single to right field that scored two runs. But in his enthusiasm, Lou rounded first base too far and got caught in a rundown. Ty Cobb raced in from center field, made the final tag, and yelled some sort of insult that really upset Gehrig.

Losing his cool and cursing Cobb, Gehrig was eventually ejected from the game by the home plate umpire. Still fuming after the game, Lou got into a fight with some of the other Tiger players, in which he fell, hit his head hard on a concrete ledge, and was knocked unconscious. When Ty Cobb started kicking Gehrig while he was down, Babe Ruth stepped in and threw a punch at Cobb.

It was reported that when Gehrig regained consciousness, he asked, "Did I win?" Although still in pain from his head injury, Lou was in the lineup the next day.

CHAPTER 8

THE COURAGE OF YOUR CONVICTIONS

*When I finally got my head screwed on straight about the streak, the bottom
line for me was simple. I fell back on the sense of conviction passed on to
me by my dad. "When you believe in something and you think it's right,
you have to be strong enough to have the courage to stand up for it."
To sit out a game at this point would not only dishonor Lou Gehrig
and the game of baseball, it would dishonor me.*

When the 1994 major league baseball season ended, I was
122 games away from Lou Gehrig's consecutive-games
record. Under normal circumstances, I would just have kept on
playing and let destiny take me wherever I was intended to go.
However, there was nothing normal about the 1994 season,
and questions and uncertainties surrounded the streak.

On August 12, 1994, the baseball season closed out prema-
turely for the first time since 1918, when World War I stopped
play. Not long after the players voted to go on strike, the team
owners canceled the rest of the season—including the World
Series, which was not played for the first time since 1904. Personally, I felt terrible about the whole thing, mainly because I

couldn't play ball. I was having a good year, too—batting .315 with 13 homers, 75 RBIs, and a .985 fielding percentage. The Orioles were playing well: Our record was 63-39, good enough for second place in the American League East. None of that mattered much, though, because players and owners couldn't get together to work out our differences. So the consecutive-games streak stopped temporarily at 2,009.

During the collective bargaining scenario, the business side of baseball reared its ugly head. I think the average baseball fan believed the strike was all about somebody wanting more money. But in my mind, it wasn't about minimum salaries. It was about preserving the free market for baseball. When the owners threatened to start the 1995 season using replacement players, things just got worse for everyone. And in my case, an unusual incident occurred. At the October players' union meeting in New York, my old teammate Mark Belanger pulled me aside for a brief chat. Mark was a special assistant to Donald Fehr, the players' association's executive director. "Cal, if you like, we can talk to the players and see how they would feel if you decided you wanted to cross the picket lines and play," said Mark. "You're an unusual circumstance."

I appreciated Mark's offer, but I didn't have to think twice before answering. "I'm on strike with the players, period," I replied. "I don't want any special treatment. I'm not going to cross any picket lines. And that's that."

But a lot of people didn't want to see the streak jeopardized. The new Baltimore Orioles owner, Peter Angelos, subjected himself to possible fines and suspensions by refusing to support the idea of replacement players. A former labor lawyer, Mr. Angelos was looking out for me, the Orioles, and his union relationship. I very much appreciated his position. But I was even more astonished when the Baltimore City Council and the Maryland state legislature both passed laws banning the use of replacement players in Camden Yards.

I was a bit concerned that the streak was being used as a bargaining chip between the players and the owners. I just didn't understand what all the fuss was about. Worst of all, the controversy about my playing in every game came up again—and I couldn't help but think about all the criticisms that I'd read ever since the streak had made its way onto the media's radar screens. That criticism had reached a crescendo a few years back when two prominent baseball guys made public statements. Tim McCarver, former Cardinals catcher and now a well-respected sports analyst, said he thought I should take a day off because the streak was hurting both my performance on the field and the Orioles as a team. And San Francisco Giants coach Bobby Bonds, a great ballplayer, went on record saying, "It's idiotic. If I were his manager, he'd be out of there. He's hurting the team and showing that personal goals are more important. He wants to break Lou Gehrig's record even if it'll cost Baltimore the pennant."

In 1937, Babe Ruth surprised everybody by criticizing Lou Gehrig's consecutive-games streak. "This Iron Man stuff is just baloney," said Ruth. "The guy ought to learn to sit on the bench and rest. They're not going to pay off on how many games he's played in a row. When his legs go, they'll go in a hurry."

I took those statements with a grain of salt. McCarver and Bonds were entitled to their opinions. However, I didn't agree that I was being selfish when I stayed in the game. Actually, I thought it would have been selfish of me to request a day off when Roger Clemens or Randy Johnson was pitching against the Orioles. In moments like those, I felt the team needed me most. And I wasn't going to be selfish enough to say to my teammates, "Hey, when those guys are pitching, you're on your own. I don't want to look bad."

I was relieved when a federal judge issued an injunction against the team owners and forced major league baseball to resume play on April 25, 1995. At least now I could stop weighing down my mind with all the talk of the streak and Lou Gehrig's record—and just get back to playing baseball.

At least that's what I thought.

However, we were given only three weeks of spring training to get ready for the regular season. When I arrived in Florida, I was hoping to ease into everything. But from day one there was elevated interest in the consecutive-games streak. I don't think the Orioles had ever experienced so many reporters, cameras, and newspeople right off the bat. It really blew me away. In my first formal interview, I said what was on my mind: "I'm going to do the best I can at retaining my focus on baseball and try to approach this season like I've done every other season. I might handle it terribly. I might handle it okay. I don't know."

As the season got going, however, I came to the realization that I didn't really know what I was getting into. People were starting to bring up issues that I didn't want to get into. How do we celebrate Ripken breaking Lou Gehrig's record? There's a scheduling problem: How can we make sure he breaks the record in Baltimore? Well, I just didn't want to hear any of that.

At first, my wife encouraged me to surrender to the process and not try to control it. She said it would allow me to go with the flow and not be constantly worried. That was good advice, and I followed it for most of the season. But I also had to come up with a way to make sure that all this attention did not disrupt my game preparation or, worse yet, become a distraction for my teammates. So I set up a routine where, at the start of every series, I would make myself available to the media early in the day. Usually, I'd go out to the dugout for an hour or so, answer all their questions—and my obligation for that three- or four-game series would be done. The rest of the time, my teammates and I could focus on baseball.

The early part of the 1995 baseball season was of concern to most baseball players around the league. Some franchises were a wreck financially. There was still tension between the owners and the players. Worst of all, attendance was down more than 20 percent from the previous year, because fans were soured by the strike. There was even talk of boycotting baseball. In the Baltimore Orioles clubhouse, we all got together and discussed it. In the end, what we decided as a team was really the only thing we could do. We decided to just play baseball.

STUBBORNNESS

When I was sixteen, a snowstorm blanketed the countryside around Aberdeen, Maryland. City snow removal didn't make it out to us very often, so my father figured he'd plow the neighborhood roads himself. My brother Billy and I drove up to the barn with him to help fire up the tractor and get everything ready to go. But when Dad went to start the engine, the battery was dead. So he went over to the tool bench, grabbed an old metal crank, and said, "Kids, I'm going to teach you how to crank a tractor."

At first, Dad put the crank in the front of the engine and turned it gingerly a couple of times in order to create some torque. But it still wouldn't start. Finally, he looked at us and said, "Look, I'm going to windmill this thing to get it started. But I never want to see you kids do it because it's dangerous." The danger Dad was referring to involved the possibility of the engine backfiring while the crank was on the way back up. If that occurred, the crank could slip and fly off. Well, sure enough, that's exactly what happened. On Dad's first turn, we heard this loud boom, and the metal crank flew straight up and cut a huge gash in his forehead. To stop the blood flow, he grabbed an old, oily rag and held it to his head.

Since I was sixteen and had my driver's license, I felt a responsibility to do something. "Get in the car, Dad," I said. "I'll drive you to the hospital." As the three of us drove off, Dad told me to pull into the driveway of our house. He disappeared inside for about five minutes and came out with a butterfly bandage on his forehead. "Okay," he said, "let's go back to the barn."

"But, Dad . . . ," I started to protest.

"C'mon. I'm all right. Let's go." So we went back to the barn, got the tractor started, and Dad plowed out all the streets in the neighborhood.

That experience sure made an impression on me. But I didn't learn until years later that the tractor crank's hitting my father in the head was nothing compared to some of the things he'd endured as a professional baseball player. Dad was a catcher who played before modern catcher's mitts were available. He was also taught to catch with two hands. So foul tips were always hitting his bare right hand, knocking off a fingernail or tearing back the skin, or breaking a bone. Earl Weaver told me that he once came out of the dugout to check on my father, saw his finger in a bloody mess, and tried to take him out of the game. "You're not taking me out of this game, Weaver," my father replied. "I'm staying."

"What are you talking about?" Earl replied. "You're finger's probably broken or something. How are you going to play like that?"

"Aww, I'll just tape these two fingers together and it'll be okay." So the trainer taped Dad's fingers and he stayed in the game.

"Nothing could get him out of there," Earl said. "He was like the hardest piece of stone on the planet."

With that kind of toughness from my father, I think you can imagine the environment in which I grew up. When I was eleven or twelve, Dad would take us over to the old high school gym during bad weather and hit us grounders. Sometimes, the ball would skip so fast on the wood floor that I couldn't get my glove down in time, and I'd get nailed on the shin. When I yelled "Ouch!" and started limping, Dad would just look at me.

"What's the problem?" he'd ask. "The ball only weighs five and a quarter ounces, for crying out loud. Get back in there. Here comes another one."

It was like that for everybody in the family, too. If one of us kids fell off a bicycle and skinned a knee, Dad would always come over and take a close look at the injury to see whether it was serious. Of course, most of the time it wasn't. So Dad would give us one of his quaint statements: "The good news is you'll be all right before you're married twice" or "You'll be all right once it stops hurting" or "Just rub a little tobacco juice on it and it'll be all right." I swear, one time I remember wondering where in the world I was going to get some tobacco juice.

When I look back on those times now, I realize that my father was teaching me a certain mental firmness and toughness. As a result, my professional attitude toward injuries was shaped from an early age. My dad's principle of "Don't let your young son whimper away just because he gets banged on the shin" turned into "If I get hit in the head by a pitch, yeah it hurts, but I can still play." That attitude was learned and conditioned over a long period of time. From Little League through the minor leagues, I played with small injuries. I had to. I mean, can you imagine me going to my father and saying something like "Dad, I have turf toe and can't play today" or "My hamstring is a little tight and I have to miss a game"?

I'm also fairly certain that I inherited some of my father's attitude. As a professional, for instance, I could rightly be described as ornery when somebody suggested I take a day off. I've also been described as stubborn. Usually, the first thing that comes into your mind when you hear the word *stubborn* is negative. But I believe my stubbornness was a positive trait that helped me persevere through my career. After all, just think of all those injuries I played through: sprained ankles, sprained knees, slipped disk, hyperextended elbows, dislocated fingers, head injuries from being hit in the head by pitched balls, and so on. However, it never occurred to me during any of my injuries to take the easy way out.

Lou Gehrig played with all kinds of injuries and maladies. He had sprained ankles, busted toes, concussions, stomachaches, backaches, and sore arms. Late in his career, Lou's hands were x-rayed and doctors determined that he had suffered seventeen assorted fractures, all of which had healed by themselves. Every one of his ten fingers had been broken at one time or another. When asked about it, Lou responded, "What's a broken finger when you're with a ball club that is fighting for a pennant?"

I also believe that the mental toughness associated with being a bit stubborn aided me in dealing with criticism. If the media questioned my approach, I stayed the course. If other players said I was being selfish by staying in the lineup, I granted their right to have an opinion, but I still stayed in the game.

I don't think it's much of a stretch to say that every manager in every organization has had an employee call in with a one- or two-degree fever and say, "I just don't feel well enough to come to work today." Sometimes, it happens when there's a particularly big day at the office, when the pressure will probably be more intense than usual. But when the chips are really down, a good manager knows he can always count on his best people to be there. I always felt, personally, that when you're a little bit sick or injured, the answer is not to take time off. The answer is to keep going. There are people counting on you. Every game is important. It's your responsibility to show up and try to help.

Brooks Robinson played in nearly 2,900 baseball games for the Baltimore Orioles. When asked if he could put into words what playing in 2,131 consecutive games meant to him, Brooks replied, "You have to be awful stubborn to do that."

Brooks was right. I was stubborn—but in a good way. Good stubborn leads to mental toughness. And mental toughness leads to perseverance. Count on it.

GOING ALL OUT ALL THE TIME

Two weeks before spring training of my second year in pro ball, I went over to the local gym to play in a basketball game with some of my buddies. I showed up early, and while waiting for them to arrive, I got into a lesser pickup game. I was just playing easy, trying not to generate a lot of contact, when, all of a sudden, I stepped on another guy's foot and blew out my ankle. The team doctors questioned whether I'd be able to start the season, so I was put on a fast-paced regimen of treatment. As I was resting my ankle in the whirlpool for the first treatment, I concluded that I'd hurt myself because I was not playing all out. If I had been playing to win that game, rather than just loafing around, I would never have landed on somebody else's foot, would never have blown out my ankle, and would never have been in danger of missing the opening of the season.

That one injury became something of a life lesson that I would apply to baseball. First, I learned to tape up my ankles properly before each and every game, figuring that they could very well be a weak point for my body. The taping gave me just a bit more support to hold my six-foot-four-inch, 225-pound frame. Second, and more important, I vowed never to let my guard down again. I was going to play all out all the time. Doing so, I reasoned, would insulate me from injury. If I had to dive for a ground ball to snag it, I would dive. If I had to slide hard into second base to break up a double play, I would slide hard. I was going to play baseball the way it was supposed to be played, which, in my mind, fit naturally into my personality on the diamond.

During my entire major league career, I never played any differently. But in 1995, leading up to my breaking Lou Gehrig's record, sports pundits talked about my style of play. They examined the issue in eight different ways, and some theorized that the way I approached baseball was conducive

Lou Gehrig always hustled on the baseball diamond. He dove for ground balls, flung himself over railings to catch foul balls, and often used his bare left hand to help him scoop bad throws out of the dirt. Nobody on the Yankees played harder than Lou.

to *not* getting hurt. Because they didn't see me running into fences very often, they figured I was taking it easy just so I could stay in the game and get the record. Well, during the middle of this media "examination" into my style of play, I was involved in a collision at home plate that ended the controversy once and for all.

In a game against Oakland on June 9, 1995, Rick Sutcliffe was on the mound for us and was having control problems. In the top of the first inning, with the bases loaded and two outs, catcher Terry Steinbach stepped into the batter's box. Sutcliffe's first pitch was a brushback, up and in. Steinbach picked himself up and scowled back at the mound. Clearly, he thought Rick had tried to intimidate him. The count went all the way to 3-2 before Terry finally struck out. Well, that really made him mad. He threw down his bat and helmet, went into the dugout, and put on his catcher's gear in a huff.

In the bottom of the first, our first two batters made outs. Then I stepped into the batter's box. Oakland pitcher Bob Welch quickly got ahead of me in the count, 0-2. I suspected there might be some sort of retaliation for Sutcliffe's knockdown pitch to Steinbach. After all, Tony La Russa was now managing the Athletics, and he definitely had that reputation.

But down two strikes, I was in no position to be thinking about getting drilled. I had to protect the plate. Sure enough, Welch threw me a pitch that I thought, at first, was a breaking ball. It kept coming, coming, coming, but when I finally realized the ball was not going to break, it was too late. At the last split second, I managed to raise my hands to the front of my face, and the ball hit me in the left hand. It didn't hurt all that much, and while I was lying on the ground, I looked at Steinbach and asked him if that was intentional. "Oh, noooo," he replied. Well, I took that as a very sarcastic response.

When I got down to first base, I was angry. I started thinking the way they used to in the old school of baseball. How was I going to get them back for that? I might be able to take somebody out on a double-play ball. Maybe I could lay a bunt down the first-base line and run into the pitcher as he tried to field it. I didn't know how I was going to do it, but I had to send a message.

After the next batter walked and advanced me to second base, I immediately thought, "Wow, wouldn't it be great if there was a play at home plate?" Well, sure enough, our next batter hit a line-drive one-hopper to right field. I knew the outfielder, Ruben Sierra, had a good throwing arm, but with two outs I was off at the crack at the bat. The third-base coach waved me home, but, in all honesty, my mission at that moment was not to score. My mission was to flatten Terry Steinbach.

Sierra made a great throw and it turned out to be a bang-bang play. The ball and I got to home plate right about the same time. Steinbach, still wearing his mask, caught it and turned his head toward me. I lowered my shoulder and hit him full force with my right bicep. We collided with such force that he was pushed back, hit his head on the ground, and rolled over. I don't know how he managed it, but Steinbach had the presence of mind to hold on to the ball. The umpire called me out, and the inning was over. I really didn't care, though. I felt no remorse, and I was still fuming as I went back into the dugout, picked up my glove, and took my position. As I was taking some warm-up grounders, I gazed over into the Athletics dugout and noticed that the team trainer had placed a towel on Steinbach's head and appeared to be giving him smelling salts. Then they escorted him through the tunnel, and a new catcher came in for the rest of the game. Just before the first pitch of the second inning, I remember looking down at the sleeve covering my right bicep. There were three parallel black lines left there from the catcher's mask. When I saw that, I said to myself, "Mission accomplished."

From my position, I also noticed that Tony La Russa was really angry. "We can play that way, too," he was yelling. "We can play hardball, too." That inning, Rickey Henderson reached first base, and the next guy up hit a fast grounder to the second baseman. We turned a quick double play, but Henderson came sliding into me at second base really late. "What was that all about?" I asked.

"Skip is really mad," Rickey replied, "so I had to make it look like I was coming after you."

I spoke with La Russa later and asked him if he had ordered Welch to throw at me. He said he did not, and I believed him. When I spoke with Steinbach the next month at the All-Star game, he admitted to me that he'd deserved what he got. Of course, I knew then that Terry had given the signal for the pitch that decked me. I didn't realize it until many years later, but Steinbach had gone on record with the media as saying that our collision had actually increased his respect for me. "A person like him, especially chasing that record the last couple of years, might be more reserved," he said. "Not him. He's very aggressive. He does what it takes to win."

The Steinbach collision pretty much ended the media examination into my style of play. "I guess Ripken isn't really playing for the streak," they wrote. "If he was, he'd be playing cautious and would have avoided that situation." Of course, the absolute truth is that I never changed my style of play. I always allowed the game situation to dictate my approach. And I always played all out.

How many people in life don't go all out? How many just go through the motions? I think the answers to those questions are pretty simple. Most people believe that they're more likely to hurt themselves if they go all out all the time. They might hurt themselves physically, or they might hurt themselves professionally. When you play hard, you tend to call attention to yourself. And there is an inherent risk in doing so. People will take notice of your performance. Those of us who fear failure or are a bit insecure do not want to call attention to ourselves.

Speaking for myself, however, I don't believe I ever felt insecure on the baseball field, and I certainly was never afraid to fail. Rather, I believe that playing all out all the time both insulated me from injury and kept me in the lineup. Physically, my hard style of play prevented me from sustaining a major injury. That was the lesson I'd learned years ago from that foolish little basketball game when I blew out my ankle. Professionally, by playing all out I attracted the attention of my managers and my teammates. And I *know* they appreciated the fact that I gave my all every single day.

It's kind of ironic in a way when you think about it. You'd think that, by playing all out all the time, I would have increased my chances for sustaining a serious injury. In fact, the opposite was true. That approach actually helped me persevere through every moment, every game, and every season. I don't think I would have broken Lou Gehrig's record if I had played any other way.

DETERMINATION

In 1995, as the baseball season progressed, media attention increased and the pressure on me began to mount. It seemed that every time I turned around, some sportswriter or television commentator was taking a new angle on the consecutive-games streak. One magazine actually asked my wife if she let me use knives around the house. "Do you let him cut up food? Couldn't he get hurt and knock himself out of the lineup?" Kelly played along in a good-natured manner: "Oh, no, I don't let him cut his own food anymore. I don't let him do other things around the house that could injure him, either."

All the attention began to distract me a little bit. I became worried that I might get obsessed with the streak, which might, in turn, cause me to play cautiously. I started to think about how Billy Williams had voluntarily ended his streak of 1,117 consecutive games in 1970 because the pressure became so intense. I thought back to my conversation with Dale Murphy at the 1986 All-Star game, where he told me why he had ended his 740-game streak for much the same reason. I also thought about a talk I'd had with my teammate Brady Anderson. When I asked him what he thought about the streak, he replied, "It's one of the greatest records in baseball history. You'll be considered one of the greatest to ever play the game." But that answer, in all honesty, made no sense to me. I was supposed to be one of the greatest players simply because I had played in all these games? No way.

Around this time, I also became concerned about media comments that my fate was out of the hands of my manager. It was too big a record to mess with, people said. Phil Regan wouldn't dare take Ripken out. Cal now had all the power. Well, I really resented the implication, because I was raised to respect my manager. In hindsight, I really don't think it had much of an impact on Phil. He treated me very well in 1995, and I felt that if there was a question about whether I should be in the lineup, he would have talked to me about it. But, at the time, a lot of crazy thoughts were running through my head.

At one point in the first few months of the season, somebody suggested that I play game number 2,130 to tie Gehrig's record, then sit out the next day. My immediate reaction to that was pretty basic: "They've got to be kidding. It wasn't about the streak to get to this point, and it shouldn't be about the streak tomorrow. It's always been about playing baseball."

Shortly before playing in his landmark 2,000th consecutive game on May 31, 1938, Lou's wife, Eleanor, suggested that he take the day off. "What challenge is there for you now?" she asked. "Why keep adding to the numbers when nobody else will ever come close? Just skip the game. Stop at 1,999."

"You can't be serious," Lou responded. "They've got a little ceremony prepared for me at the stadium today. I can't just walk out on them."

Another thing that snapped me out of my little depression was reading the dozen or so pages I had written on hotel stationery after my dad pulled me out of the lineup back in 1987 to end my consecutive-innings streak. Reading those pages made me remember how numb I'd felt sitting on the bench. I felt that I had compromised my values by coming out when I didn't really have to. Worst of all, I felt that I had let myself down.

After that, I became determined not to change my approach for anybody or anything. I even resisted the temptation to learn more about Lou Gehrig. And that was difficult, of course, because he was in the news all the time. Everybody asked me questions about him. People who had seen him play came up and told me about their experience. One fan even gave me a bat that Lou had signed. But that year, I didn't want to learn about Gehrig because I didn't want to be tempted to be like him. I thought it might disturb my normal approach to the game. Only years later did I realize our approaches to playing baseball were similar.

When I finally got my head screwed on straight about the streak, the bottom line for me was simple. I fell back on the sense of conviction passed on to me by my dad. "When you believe in something and you think it's right, you have to be strong enough to have the courage to stand up for it." To sit out a game at this point would not only dishonor Lou Gehrig and the game of baseball, it would dishonor me.

Run away from the pressure? Not me. That's not who I was. I was going to be myself. I was going to stay in the game, do my best, and let the chips fall where they may.

THE ONLY TIME I EVER felt an obligation to break Lou Gehrig's record was during the final week leading up to games 2,130 and 2,131. There was such tremendous anticipation on the part of Orioles management, my teammates, my family, and baseball fans that I just didn't want to disappoint everybody. The fact that our team had fallen out of the pennant race focused all the more attention on the streak. Of course, that just added to the pressure. I began having some sleepless nights, and leading into those final two games, I was actually running a one- or two-degree temperature. I didn't bother going to the doctor, because I knew it wasn't the flu or anything like that. I was just plain run-down.

On September 5, 1995, I tied Lou Gehrig by playing in my 2,130th game. Even though I didn't sleep well that night, I felt an overall sense of relief. Lying awake at three o'clock in the morning, I told myself that the day had finally arrived. It was now a foregone conclusion that I'd break the record. All I had to do was show up and do what I had been doing for the past fourteen years.

We all woke up at about 7:00 A.M. on the morning of September 6. At breakfast, Kelly and the kids gave me a T-shirt to acknowledge Dad's big day. "2,131 hugs and kisses for Daddy," it read. But playing in that upcoming game was not the most important thing in the Ripken household that day. This was my five-year-old daughter Rachel's first day of kindergarten. I drove her to school myself. It was just the two of us, and I'll never forget how excited she was, chatting excitedly all the way. When I pulled up in front of the school, somebody opened the car door for us, and Rachel just popped out and ran inside, barely waving good-bye to me. Then I drove back home and took a nap.

A little bit antsy, I showed up at the ballpark several hours early and went through my normal routine. I took batting practice, infield practice, joked around with the guys in the clubhouse, and in general just tried to get ready for the game.

It was apparent from the get-go, however, that this was not going to be a normal night. Fans lined up for blocks to purchase memorabilia—programs, pennants, shirts, jerseys, caps, and baseballs. The national media were present in force, treating this game on par with the World Series. ESPN was televising it nationally. Nearly fifty thousand fans poured into Camden Yards. Those present included Earl Weaver, Frank Robinson, Brooks Robinson, Joe DiMaggio, and the president and vice president of the United States. Of course, my mother and father were there, as were my brothers, Billy and Fred, and my sister, Elly. Kelly and our kids sat in our front-row box seats, and the Orioles arranged to have Rachel and Ryan throw out the ceremonial first pitches.

Our opponents that night were the California Angels, who were leading the American League West Division by five games over Seattle. We'd split the first two games of the series, and it was important for them to win this one. Going into the game, I had a fairly hot bat. Even though my average was only .266 on the year, I had been hitting .378 over the last nine games and had homered in each of the first two games against the Angels. I had actually come out of a slump after having a conversation with Mike Mussina. He'd noticed that I was a bit jumpy and encouraged me to focus on my crouch and flatten out my swing a little bit. From that point on, things just clicked for me.

As fate would have it, Mike Mussina was on the mound for us that night, which might have had a bit of a calming effect on me. In the clubhouse, as the game began, everybody treated me as if I were pitching a no-hitter. Nobody said a word about the streak. Of course, my adrenaline was really pumping. So I called on my experience in big games, just as I had done during the 1983 World Series. I knew I needed to calm myself down and not get too excited. "Just let your abilities do it," I kept saying to myself. I was trying hard not to let the enormity of the moment take me outside of what I knew I was capable of doing.

During my first at bat, I popped out to the catcher. But

when I came to the plate for my second at bat in the fourth inning, I hit a 3-0 pitch into the left-field stands for a home run. The crowd, of course, went wild. It was a thrilling moment for me. But most important, it put us ahead in the game by a score of 3–1.

Because the Orioles carried the lead into the middle of the fifth inning, the game became official, and the record was broken. As I trotted off the field and into the dugout, my teammates all congratulated me. They were shaking my hand, patting me on the back, and hugging me. The fans were all on their feet, cheering, applauding, yelling. When I came out of the dugout and tipped my hat, the ovation was thunderous.

At that moment, all eyes turned toward the warehouse just beyond the right-field bleachers. Several weeks before, the Orioles had put up a banner that counted down the games to 2,131. Every day, whenever the game became official, music would play in the background, anticipation would swell, and the banner would unfurl with the next number.

I must admit, however, when the music started and that banner went from 2,130 to 2,131, I was extraordinarily moved. It was the first time I ever got choked up about the streak. I saw all my teammates standing and applauding. The Angels were doing the same on the top step of the visiting dugout. The crowd was absolutely delirious. Fireworks were going off. Lou Gehrig's consecutive-games record, the record that would never be broken, had finally been surpassed. And to tell you the truth, I just couldn't believe it was me who had done it. At that moment, I thought about all the people who'd ever helped me in baseball—my dad, my managers and coaches, my teammates. And I felt very, very grateful. Then I went over and hugged my wife. I took off my jersey to show my son and daughter that I had worn the special T-shirt they had given me that morning. I hugged and kissed them both—and I gave Kelly my jersey and hat.

After going back into the dugout and putting on another jersey and hat, I came out for another curtain call or two. It was at this point that I looked up into the skybox where my Mom, Dad, brothers, and sister were standing. I thought about all those values we had shared growing up, about all those sibling competitions, and about my mom's recipes and advice on healthy eating. But it was when my eyes met with my dad's that I almost lost it. It seemed like there were a thousand words from father to son streaming through our hearts. I will never forget that moment.

Then I went back into the dugout and sat down on the bench next to my teammates. Rafael Palmeiro draped his arm around me, told me how proud he was of me, and encouraged me to take another curtain call. This time, I went out, waved to the fans, and touched my hand to my heart. I hoped at that moment that all the fans in Baltimore realized, through that gesture, just how much they really meant to me.

On the strength of two home runs by Rafael Palmeiro and one by Bobby Bonilla, we beat the Angels that night, 4–2. After the game, the Orioles arranged for a little ceremony to mark the occasion. I was escorted onto the field by my mom and dad, where I was flanked by family, friends, and current and former teammates.

On July 4, 1939, in response to Lou Gehrig's benching himself for, as he said, "the good of the team," the New York Yankees held a special ceremony between games of a doubleheader with the Washington Senators. More than sixty thousand fans showed up to honor Lou. On the field with him were his mother and father, his wife, his current teammates, and Murderers' Row of 1927 (including Ruth, Combs, Lazzeri, Meusel, Koenig, Dugan, Collins, Hoyt, Pennock, Moore, and Shocker). Also present at the game were Wally Pipp, Everett Scott, the mayor of New York, and the postmaster general of the United States. Everyone present knew Lou was suffering from a life-threatening disease.

Brady Anderson spoke on behalf of the Orioles players. "You have inspired many teammates," he said simply. "Your pride in and love for the game are at a level few others will ever reach. . . . We are thrilled to play beside you today . . . and we thank you for enabling us to share this wonderful moment in time."

In a surprise for the fans, Joe DiMaggio then walked out onto the field, shook my hand, and made a few moving remarks. Joe had been standing on the field that day in 1939 when Lou Gehrig had given his heartrending farewell speech in front of sixty thousand Yankee fans. "Wherever my former teammate Lou Gehrig is today," said Joe, "I'm sure he's tipping his cap to you, Cal Ripken."

Finally, it was my turn to take the microphone. I tried to keep my remarks short, but sincere. "This year has been unbelievable," I began. "I've been cheered in ballparks all over the country. People not only showed me their kindness, but more importantly, they demonstrated their love of the game of baseball. I give my thanks to baseball fans everywhere. . . . As I grew up here, I not only had dreams of being a big league ballplayer, but also of being a Baltimore Oriole. . . . For all of your support over the years, I want to thank you, the fans of Baltimore, from the bottom of my heart."

I then singled out four people to thank personally. I thanked my father for teaching me the fundamentals of the game of baseball and for teaching me to play it the right way. I thanked my mother for leading and shaping the lives of our family off the field, and for being the glue that held our lives together while we grew up. I thanked Eddie Murray for showing me how to play the game day in and day out, and for his friendship. And I thanked my wife, Kelly, who, as the most important person in my life, had enriched me with her friendship and love.

Then I mentioned Lou Gehrig: "Tonight, I stand here overwhelmed as my name is linked with the great and courageous Lou Gehrig. I'm truly humbled to have our names spoken in the same breath. Some may think that our greatest connection is that we both played many consecutive games. I believe in my heart that our true link is our common motivation: a love of the game of baseball, a passion for your team, and a desire to compete on the very highest level. I know if Lou Gehrig is looking down on tonight's activities, he isn't concerned about someone playing one more consecutive game than he did. Instead, he's viewing tonight as just another example of what is good and right about the great American game."

Then I concluded my remarks by saying, "Whether your name is Gehrig or Ripken, DiMaggio or Robinson, or that of some youngster who picks up his bat or puts on his glove, you

---

Lou Gehrig's heartfelt speech on July 4, 1939, was one of the most memorable moments in baseball history. Modestly stepping to the microphone with his head bowed and his hat in his hand, Lou kept his remarks short and sincere. Here's what he said, in part:

Fans, for the past two weeks you have been reading about the bad break I got. Yet today I consider myself the luckiest man on the face of the earth.

I have been in ballparks for seventeen years and have never received anything but kindness and encouragement from you fans.

Look at these grand men. Which of you wouldn't consider it the highlight of his career just to associate with them for even one day? Sure, I'm lucky. . . . When you have a father and a mother who work all their lives so you can have an education and build your body—it's a blessing. When you have a wife who has been a tower of strength and shown more courage than you dreamed existed—that's the finest I know.

So I close in saying that I may have had a tough break, but I have an awful lot to live for.

---

are challenged by the game of baseball to do your very best day in and day out. And that's all I've ever tried to do. Thank you."

As I walked off the field that night, I saw somebody holding up a sign that read, *We consider ourselves the luckiest fans on the face of the earth.*

EIGHT RIPKEN PRINCIPLES

8. THE COURAGE OF YOUR CONVICTIONS

1. When criticized, take it with a grain of salt. People are entitled to their opinions.
2. Stubbornness can be a positive trait in helping you persevere through some tough times. It can help you overcome injuries, and it can aid you in dealing with unfair criticism.
3. When the chips are down, a good manager knows he can always count on his best people to be present.
4. When you're a little bit sick or injured, the answer is not to take time off. The answer is to keep going.
5. You can insulate yourself from physical injury by playing all out.
6. By going all out all the time, you are likely to attract the attention of your managers and teammates. That will, in turn, make you more valuable to the organization.
7. When you believe in something and you think it's right, you have to be strong enough to have the courage to stand up for it.
8. Do not let the enormity of the moment take you outside of what you know you are capable of doing.

In mid-July 1997, I was playing third base in a game against Toronto. There were men on first and second with no outs. It was pretty clear that the Blue Jays were putting on a bunt play to advance the runners. Our defense was to have the pitcher, Mike Mussina, field the ball quickly and throw to third for the force, which meant that I would have to get back to the bag fast. The batter laid down a great bunt, and initially I had to come in because I wasn't sure Mike could get to the ball. When he did get there, I turned 180 degrees, went back to third, then turned another 180 degrees to take the throw. I caught the ball, the runner was out, and I felt this twitch in my lower back.

At home that night, I first thought that I'd twisted a hip flexor or something minor like that. But the pain gradually progressed down my left leg all the way to the bottom of my foot. It was so bad that night that I didn't get a wink of sleep. To get some relief, I tried icing my back and sitting in the hot tub—neither of which worked. At 6:00 A.M., I woke up Richie Bancells, the Oriole trainer, and told him I needed to see a doctor right away. So he quietly set up an early appointment with Dr. Charles Silverstein, our former team doctor, and asked that no one be told anything because I wanted to know what we were dealing with before everybody else did.

After undergoing X-rays and an MRI, I sat down with Dr. Silverstein and his two colleagues, Dr. Don Long and Dr. Lee Riley. "Cal, congratulations on a long run," said Dr. Silverstein. "But it's over. You've got a herniated disk at the L4 level. You need treatment and you'll be out for at least six weeks."

I paused for a moment and basically posed one simple question. "If I'm able to play, can I do any permanent damage?"

All three doctors looked at me in disbelief. "Well, this is not a nagging injury, Cal," said Dr. Riley. "You won't be able to withstand the pain."

"Well, stay with me," I continued. "Is the damage already done? Or can I make it worse? Will I not be able to walk for the rest of my life? Can I do more damage to it?"

Finally, Dr. Long looked at me and said, "No, I don't think you could do more damage to it."

"Okay," I replied. "Then I might give it a try."

From the doctor's office, I went straight to the ballpark and began working with Richie Bancells on getting the pain reduced to a level where I could play. As I was lying on the training table with ice on my back and electric stimulations hooked up to me, I remember thinking that, pain or no pain, I had to be in the lineup. The Orioles had been in first

---

place from the beginning of the season up until this point. My teammate Eric Davis had just been diagnosed with colon cancer and was out of the lineup undergoing chemotherapy. In addition, our starting second base- man, Robbie Alomar, had been placed on the disabled list. And the Yankees were starting to creep up on us in the standings. While I was thinking about all this, my manager, Davey Johnson, walked into the training room. I must have looked a mess, because when he saw me, his face turned ashen. Davey didn't have to say anything. His concerned ex- pression was all I needed to see. I knew that he hoped I would be able to play—and that, alone, made me feel better.

"What a time to get an injury like this!" I remember lamenting. I had endured all our rebuilding years, we'd finally made the play-offs the previous year, and we were now cruising toward a division championship. I was loving every minute of it. Of course, it would have been easy not to play. It would have been easy to say, "Okay, I shouldn't be playing with this injury. I'll be out six weeks. I accept that." But we were in the mid- dle of a pennant race, two of my teammates had been hurt, my manager needed me in the lineup, and I had waited too long for our team to get to this point. I was determined to do everything I could to get in the game.

When the moment of truth finally came, I struggled into my uniform and started warming up. The pain in my back was excruciating, and the nerve running down my left leg was very bothersome. I was uncomfortable in virtually any position—sitting down, standing up, running, or walk- ing. Still, I started the game and gradually eased into my position. Un- like other times in my career after I'd suffered injuries, I wasn't immediately tested on a make-or-break play. Rather, everything seemed fairly routine. A few weeks later, however, a couple of things happened that almost caused me to walk off the field for good.

On August 2, 1997 (game number 2,423 of my consecutive-games streak), in the bottom of the first inning at Oakland, Scott Brosius led off with a swinging roller that was hit right toward me. As I charged the ball, I felt that my body just wasn't working well enough for me to reach down, catch the ball, and throw to first. I wasn't able to make the play. Later in the game, somebody hit a high chopper to my left. I broke on the ball with the intent of cutting it off before it got to Mike Bordick at shortstop. But I couldn't get there, and instead of making the play, I lost my balance and fell.

In 1939, Lou Gehrig's timing was off. He wasn't as quick as he used to be in moving to and from first base. He had trouble fielding ground balls and hitting. "I'm just not feeling right," he told his manager.

Then one day in the locker room after a game, Lou lost his balance and fell down. And everybody knew something was terribly wrong with the Iron Horse.

In the wake of those two plays, I became discouraged. "Okay, I just can't do this anymore," I thought. From my position, I eyed a small door behind home plate that I knew led directly into the locker room. And for a moment, I thought that I'd just walk across the field without saying a word, exit through that door, and that would be it—the end of the streak. But then something came over me. "Okay, do this," I said to myself. "Give it one more at bat. See what it feels like when you're hitting. You never know." Sure enough, I led off the next inning with a line-drive bullet to left field, and as I ran to first base, I felt that everything was going to be all right. The next day I hit a home run to win the game. And over the next month, I went on a hitting tear, batting over .300 and getting some really big hits. Of course, the irony of the situation was not lost on me. There were all those times when my stellar fielding had sustained me despite my batting slumps, but now my hitting was keeping me in the game when my fielding was poor.

In early September, we played a big series with the second-place Yankees. I hit well in those four games and we won three of them. After that, I knew we were going to win the division, and I relaxed a little bit, both mentally and emotionally. And from September 10 to October 10, I went into the tank at the plate. I couldn't get a hit to save my life. I did regain my hitting stroke for the play-offs, though. And by then, my back was feeling much better. We defeated the Seattle Mariners in the first round of the play-offs, but lost to the Yankees (who had made the play-offs as a wild card) in the American League Championship Series.

Playing through the pain from that herniated disk in my back was the most difficult thing I had to endure during my entire 2,632 consecutive-games streak. No other injury even came close. By persevering through that situation, I believe a lot of people came to understand what I was really all about, because it really had nothing to do with the streak. I had broken Lou Gehrig's record two years before and still hadn't missed a game. So now people realized that, for me, it wasn't about setting records. I played baseball for love of the game.

AFTERWORD

Playing in 2,632 consecutive ball games and breaking
Lou Gehrig's record had nothing to do with extraordinary talent. I
didn't have a bionic body or a burning desire for the spotlight. I
I simply showed up and honored the game of baseball by
playing as well as I could as often as I could. In doing so,
I became an unintentional hero.

After breaking Lou Gehrig's record, I played 501 more consecutive games over the next three years. But on September 20, 1998, before the last Orioles home game of the season, I went to my manager, Ray Miller, and asked him to take me out of the starting lineup. I'd been experiencing back pains again. I was in a bit of a slump. And at age thirty-eight, I was just plain tired. "The emphasis should be on the team," I said. "I think the time is right."

> On Sunday, April 30, 1939, after playing in 2,130 consecutive games over fourteen years, Lou Gehrig went up to his manager, Joe McCarthy. "I'm benching myself, Joe," he said. "For the good of the team."

One out into the game, when it became apparent that I was not going to play, the players and coaches on our opposing team, the New York Yankees, walked to the top step of the visitor's dugout and started applauding. Of all the teams to end the streak against, having it be Lou Gehrig's former team was ironic and, I might add, a total coincidence. Soon the sellout crowd followed the Yankees' lead and began cheering. I stepped out of our dugout, tipped my hat toward the Yanks, waved to the crowd, and sat back down on the bench. That was it. The streak was over. I had played in 2,632 consecutive games.

> When the public address announcer ran down the Yankee lineup before the game, he paused after coming to Gehrig's normal place in the lineup. "At first base, Babe Dahlgren," he said. A hush came over the crowd as they realized that Lou Gehrig was not going to play. The crowd, the visiting players, and virtually everybody in the stadium then stood up and applauded. Having carried the Yankee lineup card out to home plate, Lou simply tipped his cap, walked back to the dugout, and sat down.

IN JUNE 2001, I announced my retirement effective at the end of the season. In every road game that year, I was cheered by fans, opposing players, and even umpires. At the beginning of each series, most of the teams held a little ceremony marking the last time I would play in their stadium. Virtually every aspect of this mini "farewell tour" was both gratifying and a bit uncomfortable. After all, I never did seek the limelight.

At my final All-Star game that year, in which I was voted starting third baseman, I homered on the first pitch I saw, and after the American League posted a 4–1 victory, I was voted MVP of the game. What a way to go out! But something else that happened during the game, a small gesture of kindness and respect, will forever remain etched in my memory. Minutes before the first pitch, the starting shortstop, Alex Rodriguez, suggested that he and I switch positions for the first inning. He had come up with this idea on his own and secured approval from the American League manager, Joe Torre. Caught off guard, and holding a large third baseman's glove, I demurred. "Oh, thanks for the offer, Alex," I said, "but I don't think so."

"No, it's okay," replied Alex. "Look over at Joe." When I looked into the dugout, Torre was flashing a big smile and giving me the thumbs-up. I still didn't want to do it, though, because I had not prepared to play shortstop that night. Finally, Alex playfully shoved me over toward his position.

"C'mon, Cal, get over there, so we can start the game," he said.

Afterward, Derek Jeter, who also hit a home run that night, best summed up why Alex made the gesture. "Cal's the reason that the taller shortstops are getting a chance to play," he said. "I remember being in Little League and playing shortstop and people saying I was too tall. The first thing I would say is 'Look at Cal Ripken.' He paved the way for us." Of course, it was actually Earl Weaver who paved the way for guys like Derek and Alex. I just did what my manager asked me to do.

All the accolades during my final year, the ceremonies, the good wishes, and the kind gestures like that of Alex Rodriguez, were truly humbling. I did not realize so many people cared so genuinely about who I was or what I had done over my career.

On June 19, 1939, Lou Gehrig's thirty-sixth birthday, the Mayo Clinic released a letter announcing the findings of its extensive medical testing. "Lou Gehrig is suffering from amyotrophic lateral sclerosis," it read. "He will be unable to continue his active participation as a baseball player."

> *"You have to get knocked down to realize how people really feel about you. The other day, I was on my way to the car. It was hailing, the streets were slippery, and I was having a tough time of it. I came to a corner and started to slip. But before I could fall, four people jumped out of nowhere to help me. When I thanked them, they all said they knew about my illness and had been keeping an eye on me."*
>
> **—LOU GEHRIG**

By the time I played in my final game on October 6, 2001, at Camden Yards, I held a number of Oriole team records, including hits (3,184), home runs (431), RBIs (1,695), runs scored (1,647), singles (2,106), doubles (603), walks (1,129), and strikeouts (1,305). I had even surpassed my childhood hero Brooks Robinson in total number of games played for the Orioles (3,001).

Many people have honored me by linking my name with Lou Gehrig. But Lou was a great, great baseball player. In four fewer seasons, he had more home runs, RBIs, doubles, and walks than I did. He also had a lifetime batting average of .340 compared to my own of .276. My on-base percentage was .340; Lou's was .447. I'm fairly certain that, had Lou not been struck down in his prime, he would have played in more games than I did, too. And he would probably have ended up with quite a few Yankee team records.

> **Lou Gehrig died on June 2, 1941. He was thirty-seven years old.**

When the 2001 major league season concluded, and I officially retired as a professional baseball player, I didn't really stop to think about what I was going to do. I already knew. All the anticipation early in my career had prepared me for this moment. I'd asked veteran ballplayers such as Jim Palmer, Al Bumbry, and Ken Singleton what they would have done differently to prepare for retirement—and I'd learned from their responses. As a result of preparing for the end at the beginning, and creating roads of opportunity, I was ready to go out on my own.

Over the next five years, as I stayed with my fundamental goal of being involved in baseball and working with children, the business built itself. So I wasn't beginning anew. I was just continuing what I'd already started. Only now, my efforts would be dedicated to my company full time. In addition, as I concentrated on the early stages of my business, I was able to apply the eight elements of perseverance and related principles I had gleaned from playing twenty-one seasons of major league baseball.

Interestingly enough, the catalyst for my business career was a gift I received on September 6, 1995, the night I broke Lou Gehrig's record. The Major League Baseball Players Association presented me with a gift of $75,000 with the stipulation that I use it to build a "field of dreams" in my hometown. I was touched that the players, all of whom had chipped in something from their own pockets, had made such a meaningful gesture. And I looked at it as an opportunity to go back to Aberdeen and parlay the gift into building a small baseball complex that my hometown and I could be proud of.

While I was still playing ball, I spent quite a bit of time looking at all the possibilities. Eventually, I decided that the best thing to do was to build a stadium and bring in a minor league baseball team. But when I began looking for property on which to build, I kept running into another group, led by Peter Kirk, that had the same idea. Peter was in the minor league baseball business: He had owned teams in Bowie, Frederick, and Salisbury (all in Maryland) and had recently sold them to Comcast. Now he was interested in bringing in an independent team to Aberdeen. When I learned that he was having some difficulty making inroads with the state and county, I suggested that we team up and work together on the project. *(6. **Trusting Relationships:** Teammates, the Competition, Management.)*

When Peter agreed, I called the governor of Maryland and asked him for help. He immediately offered his help, and the next thing I knew, the state, county, and city began to fall in line. The project came together so fast, in fact, that Peter Kirk's group hesitated a bit. Essentially, before putting a shovel in the ground, they wanted to mitigate their risk by selling sponsorships, guaranteeing seats, and having the City of Aberdeen assume more of the risk.

As the project began to drag on and on, my mother, of all people, came up to me and asked, "Cal, what's going on? Is this thing ever going to be built?" Mom's innocent question snapped me into action. I realized we had to take some risks if we were ever going to get the project off the ground, and that it was unfair to make the city of Aberdeen assume most of the risk. Eventually, Peter Kirk's group bowed out because the risk was more than they wanted to bear. So I assumed responsibility for the entire project and pushed forward on my own.

After agreeing on a design for the $21 million stadium, a public-private partnership was formed with the state (one-third), county-city (one-third), and Ripken Baseball (one-third). I knew this was risky, but I was confident the project would be a success. So committed was I, in fact, that I did not yet have a team to play in the stadium. In that sense, it really was a "field of dreams." If you build it, they will come.

In July 2001, we broke ground on Aberdeen Stadium, and in October, I officially retired from professional ball. The day after the last game of the season, I traded my baseball uniform for a business suit and went to work. I had to, because I needed to buy a ball club. (*2. A Strong Will to Succeed: An Internal Drive to Achieve, Competitiveness, Commitment.*)

Initially, I thought purchasing a team was just a matter of working out the details. But when I began to look at it in earnest, I had no idea it was going to be so hard. First of all, I did not want to be independent from the major leagues. Rather, I wanted an affiliated ball club. I had personally gone through that process, thought the minor league feeder system was all part of professional baseball, and that's what I wanted. I did not realize, however, how many hoops I would have to jump through to get it. First, there were the territorial issues, which involved both the Orioles and the Philadelphia Phillies. I also had to secure approval from the minor league association, and I had to get everyone to agree to pull a team out of the New York–Penn League.

In March 2002, I finally gained approval to purchase the Utica Blue Sox (for $3 million) and move them to Maryland as a member of the New York–Penn League. After securing an affiliation with the Baltimore Orioles (largely due to the support of Peter Angelos), I renamed the team the Aberdeen Iron Birds. From March to June, I scrambled to do everything you need to do to get a team ready to play baseball (hiring a general manager, designing uniforms, selling tickets, etc.). By the time the stadium was completed on June 17, 2002, the Iron Birds (Single-A affiliate of the Baltimore Orioles) were ready to play baseball. *(4. **Preparation:** Consistency, Personal Accountability, Increasing Your Value.)*

Shortly after completion of the stadium, as we were working on designs for the rest of the complex, I was introduced to some people at USA Baseball (the national governing body for baseball in the United States). The organization is responsible for selecting teams of professional-level players to represent the United States in various international competitions. In 2000, under the superb field management of Tommy Lasorda, their team won the gold medal at the Olympics. And in 2006, their selected team represented the United States in the first ever World Baseball Classic. Virtually every major national amateur baseball organization in America is a member of USA Baseball.

Back in 2002, however, the organization was looking to

improve their branding and visibility. Part of that effort included moving from Arizona to a more centralized location back East. When they began soliciting proposals from interested cities, I immediately thought it would be a good idea for Aberdeen, Maryland, to throw our hat in the ring. After all, we already had a first-class stadium, and we were designing a great baseball complex that could be tailored to meet the needs of USA Baseball. And certainly, Olympic-caliber baseball would be a benefit to our complex and the geographic region, in general.

When USA Baseball agreed to look at a proposal from us, I got on the phone and called the governor of Maryland, again. "I think this would be a good thing for the state," I said, "and if you think it's a good thing, then maybe we have something to talk about." The governor liked the idea and asked what he could do to help.

"Well, I only have one problem," I said. "I don't know how to go about putting together this kind of proposal in the proper fashion."

"No problem," he replied. "I'll put you in touch with my chief of staff. He'll get you going."

With direction from the Office of the Governor, I organized my team at Ripken Baseball. We spread out our resources to handle different tasks, just as we would place guys at the right positions on a baseball field. From a master planning aspect, we redesigned the entire complex to meet not only our grand vision, but also the needs of USA Baseball. We created a list of prominent developers in the area, went out and showed them our plans, and asked for their thoughts.

Our team put everything we had into it for five or six months, working long, hard hours, meeting new people, and learning new and interesting parts of the development business.

Overall, I viewed the project as a wonderful challenge to know that little Aberdeen was in competition with other high-profile cities. We actually made it into the final group being considered, along with Jupiter, Florida; Atlanta, Georgia; and Cary, North Carolina (in the Raleigh-Durham Triangle). Our presentation had some very creative ideas, and we met all the requirements from the standpoint of a baseball facility. In the end, however, it came down to guaranteeing USA Baseball certain sponsorship dollars, which we weren't willing to do. Cary, North Carolina, won out—and that's where USA Baseball is today.

When the people on my team were told that we had lost, they were depressed and discouraged. I could understand that, of course, because of all the hard work they'd put in. But I didn't feel that way at all. I was optimistic and thought the entire project was an exhilarating exercise. As a matter of fact, we submitted a bid on the design for USA Baseball's new sports complex in North Carolina. We didn't get that job, either. But in the process we connected with an engineering company that led us to the development of a new family-destination project in Myrtle Beach, South Carolina. I always felt that, in the long run, our continued perseverance would allow us to apply all the knowledge and experience we had gained from our efforts with USA Baseball. *(5. Anticipation: Reducing your Risk, Optimism, Creating Roads of Opportunity.)*

As a result of going through the USA Baseball exercise,

our vision for the complex was much clearer and more re-fined. For instance, the Camden Yards–like warehouse we planned to build was originally going to be an office building. But when we looked at the numbers, that model did not work out well. So we changed the building to a hotel—a proposal enthusiastically embraced by the Marriott Corporation. We also revised our plans to add banquet and medical facilities that would be operated through long-term partnerships with reputable organizations.

Moreover, we gained considerable experience in planning and design, which, in turn, allowed us to build several big-league-caliber youth baseball fields. We modeled them after my favorite major league ballparks, including Wrigley Field, Memorial Stadium, and Fenway Park. To top everything off, one of the developers to whom we had shown the USA Baseball proposal liked our project so much that he purchased some adjacent property and agreed to develop an avenue concept with movie theaters and active-lifestyle homes.

All along the way, we strategically tried to maintain the quality and integrity of the complex. We did not try to squeeze as many fields in as the land would allow. We strove for excellence above flashiness, and long-term value above short-term profit. Most important, we ensured that the entire complex was something that a mother and father would be proud to go to with their children. *(1. **The Right Values:** Hard Work, Excellence, Honesty, and Integrity.)*

Most people think we lost when we were not selected as the home of USA Baseball. But we really won—in experience, knowledge, and expertise. When our baseball complex is eventually completed, it will become a destination point for people in the region. Even the most conservative figures estimate that we'll attract a million visitors a year. We've already begun to reap the rewards of our hard work in that the Aberdeen Iron Birds have five complete years of sellout ticket sales—a trend that I fully expect to continue. *(8. **The Courage of Your Convictions:** Stubbornness, Going All Out All the Time, Determination.)*

For my family, the centerpiece of the entire Ripken baseball complex is Cal Sr.'s Yard, which, in my humble opinion, is the premier youth-baseball facility in the United States. It is modeled after Camden Yards (home park of the Baltimore Orioles), complete with the brick warehouse (Marriott Hotel) behind the right-field fence. This park was funded and is operated by the nonprofit Cal Sr. Foundation, created in honor of my dad. The foundation focuses on helping disadvantaged youth develop character and leadership skills through baseball. Over the years, it has provided learning programs for kids and coaches associated with Boys and Girls Clubs throughout the country.

The main reason I built Cal Sr.'s Yard and the other youth-baseball fields is because I wanted kids to experience and feel the same thing I felt when I first got to the big leagues and walked into one of those great stadiums. I wanted to bring that feeling down to disadvantaged kids who may be troubled, who may be influenced by negative factors in their neighborhoods, who may have lost any hope for their futures. Most of the kids we bring in have never been away from their homes, let alone play baseball in a new uniform or on a great field. I've seen it in their eyes. When they walk out onto one of our fields, they're wowed. It really gets their attention.

In essence, we're using baseball as a hook to get in front of kids. By providing them a baseball experience to remember, we're attempting to give them some hope. Maybe we can catch them at important decision points in their young lives. And perhaps, by seeing that there are some really good things out there, they'll choose the right path for themselves. Baseball provided that path for me many years ago. It has made all the difference in my life—and I'm just trying to give a little back.

I love being associated with kids. I always have and I always will. Through the Ripken Academy, we run thousands of kids (ages eight to eighteen) through our baseball camps and clinics each year—teaching them not only the fundamentals of the sport, but the important life lessons that baseball has to offer. *(3. **Love What You Do:** Passion, Awareness → Curiosity → Learning, Dealing with Adversity.)*

In the summer of 1999, I was approached by the Babe Ruth League about a name change they had been contemplating for some time. Originally, the Babe Ruth League was formed to provide kids with an organized program after they finished with Little League at age twelve. Since then, Little League has added a division for older kids, and Babe Ruth has added a division for younger kids. The Babe Ruth League's division for young kids was named Bambino. When league officials approached me, they asked if I'd consent to have the name changed to the Cal Ripken Division. I couldn't have been more proud to agree. Because of that honor, I'm now able to associate with and, hopefully, have a positive impact on nearly seven hundred thousand youngsters (ages five to twelve) who play baseball in the Babe Ruth League.

The Ripken Sports Complex in Aberdeen, Maryland, is close to my home so that Kelly, Rachel, Ryan, and I can spend a lot of time together there. It's also so close to my mom's house that she can drive over for a few minutes to keep an eye on Billy and me. And she does!

I'm very fortunate to have been able to realize my fundamental business goal of staying involved with baseball and working with kids. It has allowed me to keep my family together, to be happy in life, and to enjoy the journey. I just don't know what more I could ever have hoped for. *(7. **Life Management:** Physical Fitness, Achieving Balance, Enjoying the Journey.)*

Now in retirement, I look back on my career in major league baseball and I have no regrets. I enjoyed every one of the 3,001 games I played in. Today, through my business endeavors, I fill my time with things associated with baseball. And every time I pick up a glove or a bat, it immediately brings me back to some sort of joy and love. To this day, whenever I walk into a clubhouse, I feel more comfortable than when I'm in a business office.

Playing in 2,632 consecutive ball games and breaking Lou Gehrig's record had nothing to do with extraordinary talent. I didn't have a bionic body or a burning desire for the spotlight. I simply showed up and honored the game of baseball by playing as well as I could as often as I could. In doing so, I became an unintentional hero.

My brother Billy says I broke Lou Gehrig's record because I could. He was right. But I might add, on behalf of my father, that because I could, I should.

Playing every day, or always being in the game, is what I'm all about. It's who I am. My chosen profession was baseball. It fit my personality. I loved it with a passion. And when you love your chosen profession with a passion, it's easy to persevere. My advice, therefore, is pretty simple: In order to succeed, in order to make a difference, make sure that whatever you do *is who you are.*

And one more thing: Don't be afraid to go out there and give it a try. Because only then can you truly experience life and find out what you're really made of.

So get out there and get in the game.

On September 6, 1995, the night I broke Lou Gehrig's record, the fans were still going crazy a full ten minutes after the number 2,131 dropped on the warehouse wall. "We want Cal!" they began chanting. "We want Cal! We want Cal!" I took another curtain call, but the crowd kept screaming.

"Hey, you're going to have to take a lap around the stadium before we can get the game started," said Rafael Palmeiro.

"Yeah, man," agreed Bobby Bonilla. "Take a lap."

"I'm not going to take a lap around the stadium," I said. "That's ridiculous."

I did go out for another curtain call, waved to the fans, but then took my place on the bench again. I thought that was enough. It was time to resume the game. But the fans kept yelling, and my teammates kept trying to talk me into taking a lap. Finally, Rafie and Bobby picked me up off the bench, pushed me to the top of the dugout, and then shoved me toward the right-field line. "Get out of here," they said. "Take a lap." So I did. I took off.

The first guy I met was Al Bumbry, who was in his position as our first-base coach. I used to shine his shoes when I was a clubhouse boy for my dad. Al grinned, gave me a big hug, and sent me on down the line toward right field. Before that moment, I was in front of a crowd of fifty thousand. But now it was a very personal, almost one-on-one situation. I found myself shaking hands with people in the stands. As I looked into their eyes, I saw that they were smiling, crying, or grinning. Some had looks of pride on their faces. Nearly everybody I shook hands with said something to the effect of "Congratulations, buddy." "Way to go, Rip." "We love you, Cal." "We're proud of you."

After I made it all the way down the right-field line, I headed to the outfield. I shook hands with the guys on the field crew, exchanged high fives with a security guard, and passed under the 2,131 banner. I leaped in the air to slap the hands of the fans in the bleachers—and I waved to the people I couldn't reach. I kept jogging toward center field and shook hands with the players in the visiting and home bull pens. When I saw Elrod Hendricks, I grabbed his arm with both hands and thanked him. Like Bumbry, Elrod had watched me grow up in the Orioles organization. When I made it to left field, I shook hands with fans in the bleachers and ran past a sign that read, "The House That Cal Built."

As I moved down the left-field line toward third base, I slowed down a bit. Fans kept pulling me toward them. Kids, dads, and moms were slapping me on the back, shaking my hand, and hugging me. Just before I reached third base, I saw the Orioles ball girl and gave her a big hug.

Then I reached all my friends who had been placed in a special row of seats where the rain tarp usually rested. They all had a kind word, a pat on the back, or a hug for me. The next group of people I ran into were the umpires, most of whom flung their arms around me in congratulations and friendship.

Then I made it to the visitors' dugout, where all the Angel players and coaches were lined up waiting for me. This was a very special moment, because these men were my peers. Every single opposing player either shook my hand or gave me a hug. And most of their comments were heartfelt and moving. "Congratulations, Cal." "Way to go, man." "You deserve it, buddy." "We're proud to know you."

Nearing the end of my lap, I greeted the fans behind home plate. At that point, I noticed for the first time that the music playing in the background was "One Moment in Time." My brother Billy came down from the skybox to shake my hand through the net. I reached the Orioles clubhouse attendant, with whom I had pulled pranks and exchanged playful punches for years. I put my arm around him and grinned. I also shook hands with Ernie Tyler, the Orioles umpire attendant, who was marking his 2,180th straight day on the job. Next, I reached my wife and kids for one final round of hugs and kisses. Then it was back into the Orioles dugout—where I belonged. After all, we still had a game to play.

I've experienced many great moments in baseball. Catching the final out in the World Series was my most powerful moment from a purely baseball standpoint. But from a human standpoint, taking that final lap was the most powerful moment of my life. People were showing their appreciation for how I lived my life, for the person I was, and for how I played the game of baseball.

And to think, back in high school, I had to run laps as punishment for not playing up to par.

Get in the game. Do the best you can. Try to make a contribution.
Learn from the day. Apply it to tomorrow.

—CAL RIPKEN, SR.
December 17, 1935–March 25, 1999